From the Best-Selling Author of *French Braid Quilts*

JANE HARDY MILLER

French Braid
transformation

12 SPECTACULAR STRIP-PIECED QUILTS

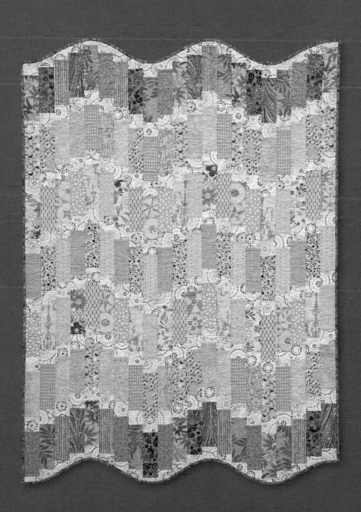

 C&T PUBLISHING

Text copyright © 2011 by Jane Hardy Miller

Photography and Artwork copyright © 2011 by C&T Publishing, Inc.

Publisher: Amy Marson

Creative Director: Gailen Runge

Acquisitions Editor: Susanne Woods

Editor: Liz Aneloski

Technical Editors: Helen Frost
                        and Joyce Lytle

Cover Designer: Kristy Zacharias

Book Designer: Kerry Graham

Production Coordinator: Zinnia Heinzmann

Production Editor: Alice Mace Nakanishi

Illustrator: Tim Manibusan

Photography by Christina Carty-Francis and Diane Pedersen of
C&T Publishing, Inc., unless otherwise noted

Published by C&T Publishing, Inc., P.O. Box 1456, Lafayette, CA 94549

Library of Congress Cataloging-in-Publication Data

Miller, Jane Hardy, 1950-

 French braid transformation : 12 spectacular strip-pieced quilts / Jane Hardy
Miller.

     p. cm.

 ISBN 978-1-60705-228-9 (softcover)

1. Strip quilting--Patterns. 2. Braid in art. I. Title.

 TT835.M5153 2011

 746.46--dc22

                         2010040913

Printed in China

10 9 8 7 6 5 4 3

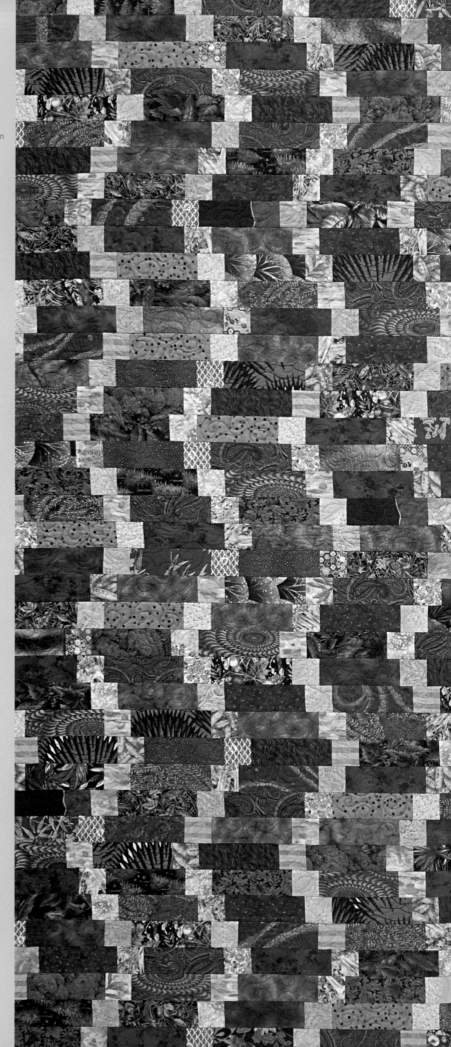

DEDICATION

This book is dedicated to quilters everywhere who, whether they're smart or silly, funny or serious, capable or careless, share the same intensity and love for quilts.

◆ ◆ ◆ ◆ ◆ ◆ ◆ ◆

ACKNOWLEDGMENTS

This book couldn't exist without my editor, Liz Aneloski, who tirelessly and instantly answered questions, and my technical editor, Helen Frost, who checked every calculation and illustration. Lois Willoughby and Stephanie Cohen tested patterns and gave me valuable feedback about the workability of those patterns, as did my students at The Quilt Scene in Miami, who seem to never tire of letting me experiment on them in classes. Patricia Ritter and Lisa Calle both worked my pieces into their busy quilting schedules, and Marta Medina enabled me to complete extra quilts by helping with the finishing. Last but never least are my coworkers and employers, who tolerate my comings and goings, both mental and physical, with barely a blink—I like to think that it's because they're used to me rather than that they don't notice a difference.

contents

Introduction 7

Preparation 8

   Tools 8

   Fabric Selection 8

   Cutting and Sewing Strips . . 9

Construction 10

   Directional Border Fabric. . . 10

   Intersecting Borders. 11

   Diagonally Pieced Columns . 12

   Using Leftovers. 14

PROJECTS

   Snake in the Grass. 16

   ◆ ◆ ◆ Bonus Project:
      Snake in the Grass—Table Runner . . . 20

   King Double Helix 22

   Lap Double Helix. 30

   The Wave 36

   The Wavelet 42

   Stax. 45

   Erector Set 51

   Quick Celtic Not. 56

   Scrappy Celtic Not. 62

   Rat Race 67

   ◆ ◆ ◆ Bonus Project:
      Amazing Maze 77

About the Author. 79

INTRODUCTION

Those of us who love strippie quilts—quilts constructed in columns instead of blocks—seem to be a minority in the quilting world. But somehow, maybe because I've been working with them for the past few years, I seem to see strippies everywhere. Even so, I didn't start out to make a bunch of quilts made from columns; they just sort of evolved. It started with wanting to make the accents in a French Braid quilt meander through the column, rather than march in a straight row; that idea became Snake in the Grass. Then I thought that maybe I could make two intertwining sets of accents in each column. Double Helix happened eventually, but on the way I was sidetracked by the Celtic Not quilts. Somewhere in there—before, after, and during—Erector Set, Stax, and The Wave occurred. Rat Race, the only project in the book actually made from blocks, was a quilt I had adapted several years ago from a traditional block. It's included here because it looks as if it's made in columns—or at least as if it should be!

I'm also a longtime maker and lover of scrap quilts, which is why there are so many in this book. There's always something new to see in a scrap quilt, and it's fun to recognize fabrics that are old friends (sometimes *very* old friends) from previous projects.

The simplest project is Stax, which can be easily constructed, even by a beginning quilter. The more complicated projects don't rely on knowledge gained in the easier ones, so feel free to dive in at the deep end if you feel confident. My wish for you is that you'll have as much fun with this book as my students and I have had testing the projects.

Preparation

TOOLS

Most of the quilts in this book are constructed in columns rather than in blocks, but that doesn't mean that you need any unusual supplies. Rotary cutting equipment is essential—keep your fingers out of the way and close the cutter when not in use—and a few of the projects require long, wide, or large square rulers. A reliable sewing machine with a consistent straight stitch and a new needle is important, as are good-quality cotton thread and fabric. A ¼" presser foot is needed for most projects—the pieces won't always fit if your seam allowance is incorrect.

The ability to follow instructions is at least as important as the products you use. The cutting instructions for many of the scrappier quilts are based on cutting from fat quarters, which means that the width of fabric (abbreviated "wof") is really a half-width, or 20+ inches. Please carefully read the instructions for your chosen project to make sure you cut strips of the correct size.

You may feel that some of the quilts from fat quarters require a lot of yardage, and you're right. Suggestions for using the leftovers will be discussed in the next chapter. But if you're cutting from fat quarters, which is an option for many of the quilts, you're usually making a scrappy quilt. To get the multifabric look that defines the genre, you need a large variety of fabrics. Just remember that you don't have to cut all the strips from fat quarters—read the cutting instructions to find the total number of strips you need and cut some or all from scraps if you prefer.

FABRIC SELECTION

Most of us have seen a few ugly quilts, and at least one was probably a scrap quilt in which the maker attempted to use every available piece of fabric. These quilts often make us think that we don't like scrap quilts. But the problem isn't that the quilt was made from scraps; the problem is that the scraps weren't used to their best advantage.

The first step in choosing fabric for a quilt is usually the selection of a main fabric, followed by the choice of coordinating fabrics—a process that works well when purchasing yardage. Scrappier quilts, however, usually rely more on consistency of color and value placement for their overall effect. This doesn't necessarily make the fabric selection process harder; in fact, in some ways it's easier, because you don't have to worry that a particular blue is a shade different than the blue in your main fabric. But scrap quilts are a true example of more being more: the more variation in shade, size, density, and style of print, the better. This style of quilt needs variation to add visual interest, as well as to simplify its eventual layout—the more fabrics you have, the less likely one is to appear next to itself later. That said, you do need a constant—whether it be a color family or relative value placement (where you put the lights and the darks)—within the pattern.

Using a liberal definition of color within your chosen color parameters will add spark to your quilt. For example, in *Double Helix Citrus* (page 22), the background fabrics are from a green to teal palette, medium-dark in value. But if you look carefully, you can see that the teals edge into truer blues, and some of the greens are grayish and more medium in value. This makes the background more interesting than it would be if all the background fabrics were more similar. After all, if they all looked the same, you could just use one fabric and make both fabric selection and cutting easier.

CUTTING AND SEWING STRIPS

When cutting strips from yardage or fat quarters, cut the largest first; if you make a mistake, you can usually salvage at least one smaller strip from it. When sewing strips together, try to align them all at one end, so you don't waste a half-segment at each end.

Cutting from actual scraps can be more time-consuming because few are the same size. First cut the smallest strips from the smallest scraps; then cut the next larger size strips from the larger scraps. If you can cut more than one size from a piece, do so. If you cut some pieces lengthwise and some crosswise, that's fine. Read the cutting instructions to determine the total number of pieces you need. But remember that you may not always have the required fabric width, so cut a few extra strips of each size. Keep a running tally of the number you cut of each size.

Because scrap strips are often different lengths, strip piecing also becomes more complicated. You have several options: Match similar strip lengths, even if they're not full width, or piece shorter lengths together to obtain the required width. A seam in the middle of a patch is often unobtrusive if the fabrics are similar, or it can be interesting if they're not. If you prefer not to seam, cut the longer pieces down to the length of the shorter pieces; match their remainders to additional shorter strips or cut them into smaller single pieces. When sewing a lengthwise strip to a crosswise one, you can minimize creepage by placing the lengthwise strip on top as it travels under the needle.

Remember, it's not that you're working with scraps but how you use them that counts.

Detail of *Double Helix Citrus* (full quilt on page 22)

Construction

*V*ery few specialized techniques are required to construct these quilts. Use your favorite methods of appliqué and border application. Border yardages do not allow for mitering, so buy accordingly.

DIRECTIONAL BORDER FABRIC

Most quilters have used directional fabric in their borders without hesitation, since there's usually no right side up to a quilt anyway. Occasionally, you might want the print in all four borders to face the same direction.

This means that you will cut two borders lengthwise (parallel to the selvages) and two crosswise (selvage to selvage), so you must purchase extra fabric. However, the amount of extra will vary depending on the size of the quilt and the pattern repeat in the border fabric. Unless the quilt is quite small, you will have to piece one set of borders, usually the top and bottom. When doing so, you have two options.

The first option, which usually works best for medium-size quilts, is to purchase enough fabric for the length. Cut the lengthwise borders first; then, from the remaining width, cut enough crosswise strips to piece the crosswise borders. The best effect is obtained by piecing so that the fabric pattern matches perfectly, appearing as a continuous design (*Double Helix Royal*, at right), but this usually means wasting fabric between repeats. You can also try to seam the border strips in a place where the noncontinuous pattern isn't so obvious (*Erector Set Brights*, at right).

Detail of *Double Helix Royal* (full quilt on page 30). Top and bottom borders appear to be a continuous piece of fabric.

Detail of *Erector Set Brights* (full quilt on page 51). Piece borders as inconspicuously as possible.

The second alternative, which is best for very small or very large quilts, is to buy enough fabric for the length *plus at least* two border widths (or four for very large quilts). First cut two (or four) crosswise borders from the full width; then cut the lengthwise borders. You will end up with a lot of leftover fabric; cut whatever crosswise borders you still need from the leftovers and add them to the full-width pieces.

INTERSECTING BORDERS

Several quilts in this book have inner borders that extend to the quilt's edges (*Snake in the Grass—Pink*, page 16). Although these borders may appear to be complicated, in some respects they are easier than standard lapped or stacked borders. Assume finished inner borders of 1" and outer borders of 5" for this example.

Detail of *Snake in the Grass—Pink* (full quilt on page 16)

1. Measure the width of your quilt top across the horizontal center and the length down the vertical center.

2. For the top and bottom borders, cut 2 outer borders the exact width of the quilt top by the outer border width (5½").

3. From the outer border fabric, cut 4 squares the same size as the outer border width (5½" × 5½").

4. Cut 4 pieces of inner border fabric the width of the outer border by the width of the inner border (5½" × 1½").

5. Sew an inner border strip from Step 4 to each end of each outer border from Step 2. Sew an outer border square from Step 3 to the other side of each inner border strip. Press all the seams toward the squares.

Attach corner squares.

6. Measure the length of your top and bottom borders; cut 2 pieces of inner border fabric that length. Sew a piece to a long side of each border. If your outer border fabric is directional, decide which direction each border will face before attaching the inner border. Press the seams toward the inner borders and set aside.

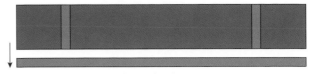

Add inner border strip.

7. If you have sewn all your border strips into 1 long piece, cut off a piece that is twice the length of the quilt top (Step 1) plus 2"–3" for the side borders. If your borders are already in 2 pieces, cut 2 outer border pieces the length of your quilt top (Step 1) plus 1"–2". (If your outer borders are directional, use 2 separate pieces and check the orientation before attaching the inner borders.)

8. Seam together enough inner border strips to obtain the required length(s). Sew an inner border strip to 1 long edge of each outer border. Press toward the outer border.

9. Trim the 2 side borders to the length found in Step 1.

10. Sew the side borders to the quilt top, matching the ends and centers. Press the seams toward the borders.

11. Sew the top and bottom borders to the quilt top, matching the ends and centers. Make sure that the seamlines of the vertical inner border strips in the top and bottom borders align with the inner border seams of the side borders. Press the seams toward the outer borders.

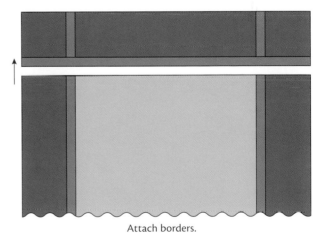

Attach borders.

DIAGONALLY PIECED COLUMNS

Several of the patterns in this book include columns that are pieced diagonally. As a result, their edges are zigzagged and must be straightened before being attached either to lattices or to each other. You will need a rotary cutter and mat and a pencil—mechanical pencils are best for keeping a sharp point. A 24" ruler at least 6" wide is also necessary, and a square ruler at least 12" × 12" is useful but not required (24" × at least 7½" and 14½" × 14½" are needed for all Celtic Not quilts).

Marking and Trimming Zigzag Edges

1. Press a column carefully and lay it out on your mat with the points of 1 zigzag edge on a line. If you are trimming a Celtic Not column, one set of zigzags is narrower than the other; use the wider set. If the column is longer than your table, accordion fold the column at one end and unfold as you work.

2. Using a wide ruler and the vertical center of the column as a reference point, measure out to the closest zag (concave corner). This is usually 5½"–5¾" for the Snake in the Grass and Double Helix quilts or 7"–7¼" for the Celtic Not quilts.

3. Find the line on your ruler that corresponds with the number you found in Step 2; place it on the column's vertical center. (It may be helpful to mark the ruler line with a piece of tape.) A long edge of your ruler should now extend down the column's outer edge. This will eventually be your cutting—not sewing—line, so it's okay if the edge of the ruler extends a thread or so past the fabric edge. If you will not add vertical lattices, trim about 12"–14" of the length at a time. If you intend to add lattices, use a pencil to mark along the ruler's full length. When marking or cutting, move your ruler hand down the ruler along with the pencil or cutter in the other hand, pressing the ruler down between the seams.

Align ruler with vertical center of column.

4. Before moving the column, use a large square ruler to mark or trim the opposite edge. To do so, double the number from Step 2 and measure across from the line you just drew. If you don't have a square ruler large enough, repeat Step 3 for this second edge of the column. If the ruler edge for this second line falls too far off the edge of the column, start again with Step 3 and move both lines ¼" closer to the center.

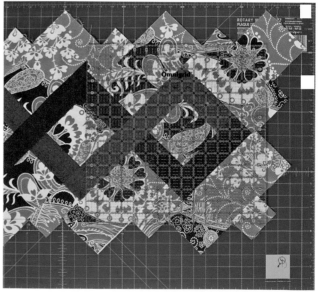

Use large square ruler to mark or trim second edge.

5. Continue down the column and mark both edges before moving on to the next section. If your marked line doesn't meet the end of the ruler after you move it, move the ruler back up the column until it does, realign it with the center of the column, and re-mark.

6. After you have marked both edges, trim the ends of the columns. Both ends must be at right angles to either the marks or the cut edges. Place the ¼″ line of your ruler at the point of the last accent; align the ruler lines that fall at the sides of the column with the trimmed edges or marked lines. Cut.

Trim ends of columns.

7. Staystitch the cut ends about ⅛″ from the edge. If you have trimmed the sides of the column, staystitch those also.

8. Mark the horizontal center of each column on both long edges by finding the center of a design element. This will be either the outermost or innermost part of the intertwined pieces on the Celtic Not and Double Helix quilts. If you are making one of the Snake in the Grass quilts, it's easiest just to count the accents, divide by 2, and count back from either end.

9. If you are adding lattices, go to the next section (Adding Lattices). If not, match the ends and centers of pairs of pieced columns and sew, pinning at least at every seamline. Then sew the units into a top.

Adding Lattices

The columns from the Snake in the Grass, Quick Celtic Not, and Double Helix quilts can be sewn together with lattices or without (*Snake in the Grass—Pink*, page 16). A lattice may be a single strip of fabric (*Celtic Not Wedding Quilt*, below), three strips of fabric (*Quick Celtic Not—Green*, page 56), or pieced fabric (*Double Helix Royal*, page 30). Before continuing, first construct the lattices by following the directions specific to your chosen project. If you are making a pieced lattice, you won't have the option of trimming it to another length in Step 2, so make sure your seam allowances are accurate.

Detail of *Celtic Not Wedding Quilt* (full quilt on page 62)

Detail of *Quick Celtic Not—Green* (full quilt on page 56)

Detail of *Double Helix Royal* (full quilt on page 30)

1. Press each column carefully and measure it down the center from end to end. Write down the numbers.

2. If the column lengths are not all the same, average them and round up to the nearest ¼". Cut all the lattice pieces this length and mark their centers. If you later add length-wise borders before the crosswise ones, use this number for those also.

3. Place a lattice strip on top of a pieced column, with right sides together and ends and centers matching. Align the long edge of the lattice strip with the pencil line on the pieced column. Pin at least at every seam.

4. Sew the lattice to the pieced column at a moderate speed, using the lattice edge as a guide for your ¼" presser foot.

5. Use a ruler and a rotary cutter to trim the zigzag edges even with the lattice edge.

6. Repeat Steps 1–5 with the remaining lattices. If your pieced columns are directional, be sure to sew each lattice strip to the same (left or right) edge. Sew these units together into pairs and then into a top.

USING LEFTOVERS

Some quilters throw away that last 3" of fabric. If, like me, you can't stand to waste those leftover pieces, here are a few suggestions. If the quilt requires many different-sized pieces, you may have enough for another project (see Snake in the Grass—Table Runner, page 20, and Amazing Maze, page 77). If not, you've created scraps, and that means more scrap quilts. If you don't make scrap quilts, smaller pieces can be used in appliqué projects.

My favorite use for leftovers is piecing them into the back, which often allows me to buy one less length or width of backing fabric. Although this process is more time-consuming than just sewing together two pieces of fabric, it makes a nice surprise when the quilt is turned over.

Back detail of *Stax Cranes* (full quilt on page 48)

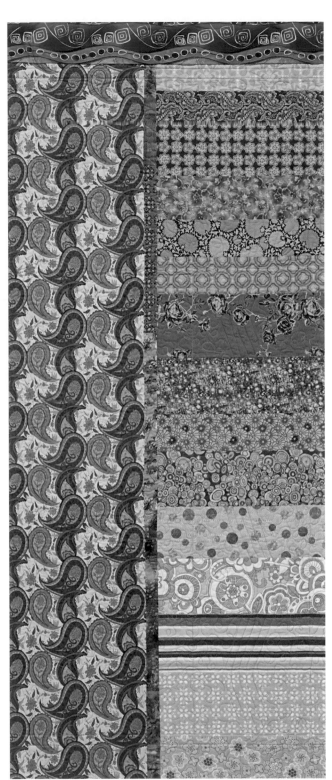

Back detail of *Snake in the Grass—Pink* (full quilt on page 16)

Snake in the Grass

Snake in the Grass—Pink, 56" × 74"

*T*his quilt sent my journey with French Braid quilts in a new direction. I designed it after wondering if it was possible to make a French Braid quilt with meandering accents rather than a straight line of them. For an entire week I would stop in the middle of a sentence, my eyes would glaze over, and I would search frantically for a scrap of paper upon which to draw a sketch. The use of several fabrics for the accents adds variety and interest.

FABRIC

Background: 18 fat quarters

Accent: 5 fat quarters*, all similar in color and value, to contrast with the background fabric

Inner border: ⅜ yard

Outer border: 1⅞ yards cut lengthwise *or* 1¼ yards cut crosswise

Backing: 3½ yards pieced crosswise *or* 4½ yards pieced lengthwise

Binding: ¾ yard

Batting: 60″ × 78″

Three fat quarters will yield enough strips; five will make it scrappier.

CUTTING

All strips are width of fat quarter (20″+) unless otherwise noted.

Background

Strip sizes are identified by their lengths throughout the instructions; separate and label each length.

◆ From each of 10 fat quarters, cut 1 strip 8½″ and 1 strip 6½″, stacking into smaller groups if desired.

◆ Divide the remaining 8 fat quarters into 2 groups of 4 each.

From each of 4 fat quarters, cut 1 strip 9½″ and 1 strip 1½″.

From each of the remaining 4 fat quarters, cut 1 strip 7½″ and 1 strip 1½″.

Accent

◆ Cut 4 strips 2½″ from each. You will use 16.

Inner border

◆ Cut 7 strips 1½″ × wof* (40″+). Seam end to end to make 1 long strip.

Outer border

◆ Cut 4 strips 5½″ × length of fabric.

Subcut 2 squares 5½″ from *each* of 2 border strips (4 squares).

or

◆ Cut 7 strips 5½″ × wof.

Subcut 4 squares to 5½″.

Seam the remaining strips end to end to make 1 long strip.

* wof = width of fabric

CONSTRUCTION

As you make the units, set them aside and label them (A, B, Br, etc.). Background fabric is referred to as BG.

Strip Piecing and A Units

1. Sew a 2½″ accent strip to each 9½″ BG strip, matching the long edges.

2. Sew the corresponding 1½″ BG strip to the other long edge of the accent strip. Press the seams toward the 9½″ strip.

3. Subcut each strip into 8 segments 2½″ wide. Label them 9½″ segments. If you can't cut 8 pieces from every fabric, don't worry; you have a few extras.

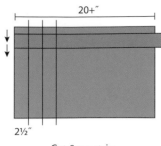

20+"

2½"

Cut 8 per strip.

4. Repeat Steps 1–3, substituting the 7½" and 1½" BG strips. Label them 7½" segments.

5. Select 4 of the 6½" BG strips and 4 of the 8½" BG strips. Sew an accent strip to a long side of each. Press seams toward the larger strips.

6. Subcut the 6½" strips and the 8½" strips into 2½" segments. Cut 8 per strip.

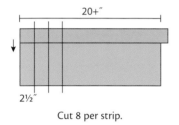

20+"

2½"

Cut 8 per strip.

7. Subcut each of the remaining 6 BG 6½" strips and 6 BG 8½" strips into 2½" segments. Label the unaccented 8½" segments A.

B Units

8. Sew an unaccented 6½" segment to the right edge of 16 of the 6½" accented segments, matching the accent end to the end of the unaccented segment.

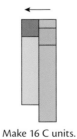

Sew 6½" units.

9. Add an accented 7½" segment to the left edge of the accented 6½" segment in each of the pairs from Step 8, matching the accented ends. One end of the unit will be even, and the other end will be stairstepped. Press all the seams toward the shortest segments. Make and label 16 of these B units.

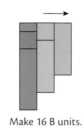

Make 16 B units.

10. Repeat Steps 8 and 9, reversing the positions of the unaccented 6½" and accented 7½" segments. Make and label 12 reverse B (Br) units. Press seams toward the shortest segments.

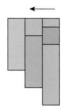

Make 12 Br units.

C Units

11. Sew an accented 8½" strip to the left edge of 16 of the accented 9½" segments, matching the accented ends, to make C units. Press seams toward the shorter segments.

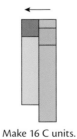

Make 16 C units.

12. Repeat Step 11, reversing the position of the 8½" and 9½" strips. Make 12 reverse C (Cr) units.

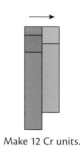

Make 12 Cr units.

Laying Out Columns

13. Starting at the bottom left end of the column, lay out sections as follows, alternating sides of the column with each unit: A, B, C, A, Br, Cr.

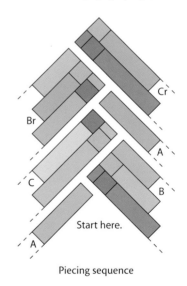

Cr

Br

A

C

B

Start here.

A

Piecing sequence

14. Add an A unit and repeat the entire sequence from Step 13 twice more for each column. Then lay out the other 3 columns.

15. When you have completed the 3 sequences, increase each column length by half a sequence by adding 1 A unit, 1 B unit, and 1 C unit.

16. Rearrange the units as desired, exchanging B for B units, Cr for Cr, and so on. The A units are easiest to change because you have more extras and because they aren't limited to one side of the column. Try to identify the more obtrusive fabrics and distribute them evenly over the top.

17. When you are satisfied with the arrangement, you will construct and place a D unit at the bottom of each column.

D Units

18. Sew a leftover unaccented 6½" piece onto the accented end of an accented 6½" piece at right angles. Make 4 of these D units. Press the seams toward the unaccented 6½" piece.

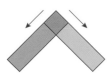

Make 4 D units.

19. Add 2 leftover A units to each side of each column top, aligning as shown.

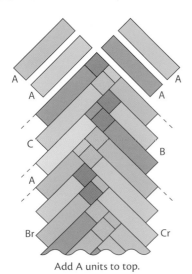

Add A units to top.

20. Sew the units into columns, beginning with a D unit. Alternate the sides to which you add units and work up toward the top of the column. Press the seams toward the newly added unit after each addition.

ASSEMBLY

21. Measure and trim the sides and ends of the columns (pages 12–13). To find the vertical center of a column, start at either end. Count up to the fifth accent square; mark. Resume counting with #1 for the following square and mark the #4 square. Continue counting and marking in this manner until all the #4 squares are marked. These squares and the end accents are the center of the strip.

22. Sew the columns together, matching the ends and each seamline. The seam allowances face the same direction when they meet, so pin at least once at each seam.

23. Add borders (page 11).

24. Layer, quilt, and bind.

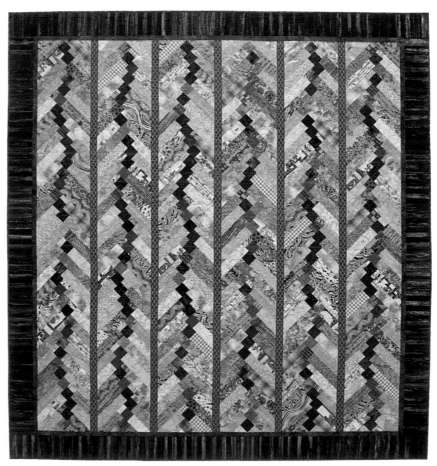

Snake in the Grass—Diamondback, 85½" × 91"

11″ × 53¾″

BONUS PROJECT:
Snake in the Grass—Table Runner

*Y*ou will have leftover segments when your
Snake in the Grass top is finished. If you
don't use them on the back of your quilt,
you may be able to make them into a table runner.

FABRIC

Patchwork: Leftover pieces from
Snake in the Grass (These were from the
Diamondback variation, page 19.)

Backing: 1 yard

Binding: ½ yard

Batting: 15″ × 58″

You will need 4 A units, 2 B units, 4 Br units,
2 C units, 4 Cr units, and a few squares. See
Construction (pages 17–19).

1. Make a center segment by sewing a 2½" background square to each side of a 2½" accent square.

Center segment

2. Cut down 2 Br units to 6½" squares by trimming off each unit's stairstep edge.

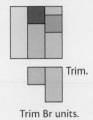

Trim.

Trim Br units.

3. Sew a trimmed Br square from Step 2 to each side of the center segment.

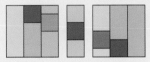

Sew Br squares to center segment.

4. Add a Cr unit to each of the 2 longer sides.

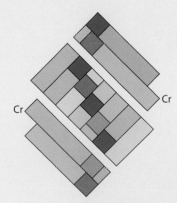

Cr

Cr

Cr

Add Cr units to center.

5. Add units to both ends in the following order, alternating sides: A, B, C, A, Br, Cr. If you don't have that many units left over, either stop after the C units or use the leftover fabric to make more units.

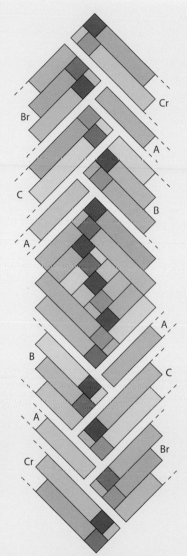

Add units to both ends of center.

6. Layer and quilt. Then trim the side edges and bind.

King Double Helix

Double Helix Citrus, 101″ × 97″, quilted by Lisa Calle

*T*his quilt involves a bit of sewing and a few seams to match, but none of this work is especially difficult. The quilt in the photo was made from scraps. The fabric requirements ask for fat quarters, which will still give you enough variety to obtain a similar scrappy look. However, you may prefer to use one nondirectional background fabric instead. The two accent colors should be similar in value and intensity, and both should contrast with the background.

FABRIC

Background: 26 fat quarters in 1 color *or* in 2 closely related colors, *or* use 5¼ yards of 1 fabric

Color #1: 7 fat quarters*

Color #2: 7 fat quarters*

Outline lattice, inner border, and optional binding: 2⅝ yards

Center lattice and outer border: 3 yards

Backing: 8¾ yards, pieced lengthwise

Binding (if different from lattice and inner border): ⅞ yard

Batting: 105″ × 101″

Five fat quarters will yield enough strips; seven will make it scrappier.

CUTTING

Background from fat quarters

All strips are width of fat quarter (20″+).

You need a total of 12 strips 5½″, 33 strips 4½″, 10 strips 3½″, 32 strips 2½″, and 12 strips 1½″. Separate and label the various sizes.

◆ From each of 8 fat quarters, cut 1 strip 4½″, 1 strip 2½″, and 1 strip 1½″.

◆ From each of 7 fat quarters, cut 1 strip 5½″, 2 strips 4½″, and 1 strip 2½″.

◆ From each of 6 fat quarters, cut 1 strip 4½″, 1 strip 3½″, 2 strips 2½″, and 1 strip 1½″.

◆ From each of 5 fat quarters, cut 1 strip 5½″, 1 strip 4½″, 1 strip 3½″, and 1 strip 2½″.

You will have a few extra strips of some sizes.

or

Background from yardage

All strips are width of fabric (40″+).

◆ Cut 6 strips 5½″, 17 strips 4½″, 5 strips 3½″, 16 strips 2½″, and 6 strips 1½″.

Subcut all strips in half at the center so they measure 20″+ by their respective widths.

Colors #1 and #2

◆ Cut 5 strips 2½″ × wof*, for a total of 35 of each color.

You will use 33 of each color.

Outline lattice and inner border

◆ Cut 10 strips 1½″ and 4 strips 2″, all × *length* of fabric.

You will have enough fabric left for binding.

Center lattice and outer border

◆ Cut 4 strips 6½″ and 5 strips 2½″, all × *length* of fabric.

* wof = width of fabric

CONSTRUCTION

Press each seam as you go. Seams may be pressed in either direction except where otherwise noted. Background fabric is referred to as BG throughout, color #1 is orange, and color #2 is yellow. Make a note of your colors, and label and set aside each unit as you cut. There are no O units. In Steps 9–12, I sometimes use the same fabric on both sides of the color #1 or #2 square. However, using 2 different backgrounds adds interest.

2½″ Squares and 4½″ Sets

1. Select 12 BG 2½″ strips and cut them into 96 squares 2½″ × 2½″. Label them F.

2. Select 7 BG 4½″ strips and 7 strips of color #1. Seam each BG strip to a color #1 strip, matching the long edges. Press toward the larger strips. Subcut 54 segments to 2½″. Label them G.

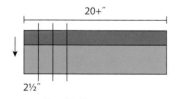

Cut 54 G segments.

3. From a strip of color #1, cut 6 squares 2½″ × 2½″. Select 6 G segments. Sew a color #1 square to each segment as shown. Press both seams toward the 4½″ segment. Label them H.

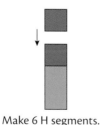

Make 6 H segments.

4. Select 6 more G segments. Sew an F square to the color #1 square on each segment as shown. Press both seams toward the BG square. Label them I.

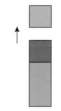

Make 6 I segments.

5. Select 7 BG 4½″ strips and 8 color #2 strips. Sew and cut as in Steps 2–4, using color #2 instead of color #1. Label them J, K, and L.

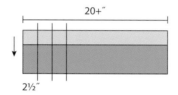

Cut 54 J segments.

Make 6 K segments.

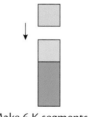

Make 6 L segments.

6. Subcut the 19 remaining 4½″ BG strips into 150 segments 2½″. Label them M.

5½″ Sets and 3½″ Sets

7. Select 6 BG 5½″ strips and 6 color #1 strips. Seam each BG strip to a color #1 strip, matching the long edges. Press. Subcut 48 segments to 2½″. Label them N.

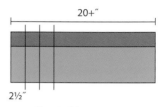

Cut 48 N segments.

8. Select 6 BG 5½″ strips and 6 color #2 strips. Sew and cut as in Step 7. Label them P.

9. Select 6 N segments. Sew the color #1 end of each segment onto a 1½″ BG strip. Recut the segments to include the 1½″ pieces. Label them Q.

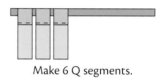

Make 6 Q segments.

10. Select 6 P segments from Step 8. Sew and cut as in Step 9. Label them R.

11. Select 5 BG 3½″ strips, 5 BG 1½″ strips, and 5 color #1 strips. Sew each color #1 strip between a 5½″ and a 1½″ BG strip, matching the long edges. Subcut 36 segments to 2½″. Label them S.

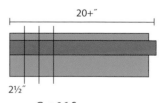

Cut 36 S segments.

12. Select 5 BG 3½" strips, 5 BG 1½" strips, and 5 color #2 strips. Sew and cut as in Step 11, using color #2 instead of color #1. Label them T.

Nine-Patches

13. Select 10 BG 2½" strips and 5 color #1 strips. Sew each color #1 strip between 2 BG strips, matching the long edges. Press seams toward the BG strips. Subcut 36 segments to 2½". Label them U.

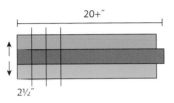

Cut 36 U segments.

14. Select 10 BG 2½" strips and 5 color #2 strips. Sew and cut as in Step 13, using color #2 instead of color #1. Label them V.

15. Select 9 strips of color #1. Sew the long sides together into 3 sets of 3 strips each. Press seams toward the center strips. Subcut 18 segments to 2½". Label them W.

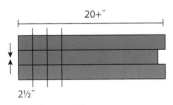

Cut 18 W segments.

16. Select 9 strips of color #2. Sew and cut as in Step 15, using color #2 instead of color #1. Label them X.

17. Select 24 M segments. Sew them into 12 pairs, stitching the long edges together. Label them Y.

Make 12 Y units.

18. Select 84 M segments and 84 F squares. Sew an F square to each M segment as shown. Label them Z.

Make 84 Z units.

A Units

Instructions are for 1 unit. Make 6.

19. Sew the right edge of an H segment to the left edge of an L segment, matching edges and butting seams. Use in Step 21.

20. Sew the right edge of an R segment to the left edge of a J segment, matching the top edges. The seams and bottom edges will not match.

21. Sew the left edge of the segment from Step 20 to the right edge of the segment from Step 19, matching top and bottom edges. The seams will not match.

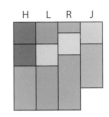

22. Sew a Y unit to the color #1 edge of the unit from Step 21, matching the top edges and seams. Re-press the seam in the Y unit if necessary to butt the seams.

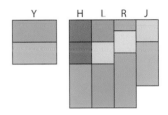

23. Sew the 4½" edge of a Z unit to the color #2 edge of the unit from Step 22, matching the top edges. Set aside.

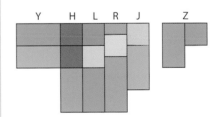

E Units

An E unit is an A unit with the color #1 and color #2 placements reversed. Instructions are for 1 unit. Make 6.

24. Sew the right edge of a K segment to the left edge of an I segment, matching edges and butting seams. Use in Step 26.

25. Sew the right edge of a Q segment to the left edge of a G segment, matching the top edges. The seams and bottom edges will not match.

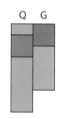

26. Sew the left edge of the unit from Step 25 to the right edge of the unit from Step 24, matching top and bottom edges. The seams will not match.

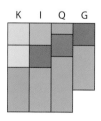

27. Add Y and Z units as in Steps 22 and 23.

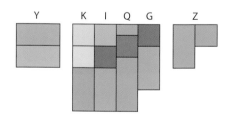

C Units

Pay close attention to the color placement when making the C and D units. Instructions are for 1 unit. Make 18.

28. Sew a U segment to *each* long edge of an X segment to construct a nine-patch.

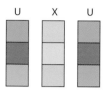

29. Sew the left edge of a G segment to the right edge of an S segment, matching top and bottom edges. Make 36.

30. Sew the 4½" edge of a Z unit to the G edge of each unit from Step 29.

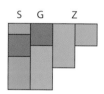

31. Sew a unit from Step 30 to each side of a nine-patch from Step 28, orienting them as shown. *Make sure* that the center strip of the nine-patch with the 3 squares of color #2 is parallel to the seams you are sewing.

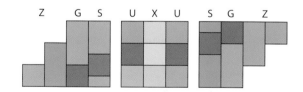

D Units

A D unit is a C unit with the placement of colors #1 and #2 reversed. Instructions are for 1 unit. Make 18.

32. Use V and W, and then T, J, and Z units to repeat Steps 28–31, reversing the colors as shown.

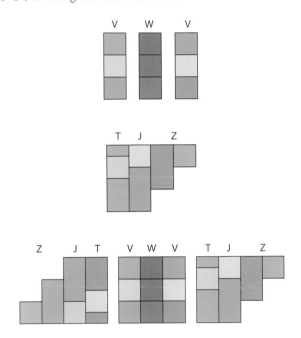

B Units

Instructions are for 1 unit. Make 42.

33. Sew the color #1 end of an N segment to either end of an M unit. Sew the color #2 end of a P segment to the other end of the M unit.

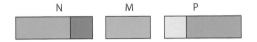

ASSEMBLY

You are making 6 columns, each beginning with an A unit and ending with an E unit. If possible, lay out all the columns before you sew. Otherwise, lay them out one at a time.

34. Lay out an A unit so the long straight edge is at a 45° angle. Add a B unit, stairstepping up half the width of the adjacent accent (1"). You can either measure and mark the center of the accent or just estimate.

35. Add a C unit, stairstepping half of an accent square in the same direction. Turn a B unit 180° (Br) and add it; then add a D unit, stairstepping as before. Continue adding units in the same order (B, C, Br, D) until you have 3 complete sequences. Then add a B unit and an E unit. Rearrange the units until you are satisfied.

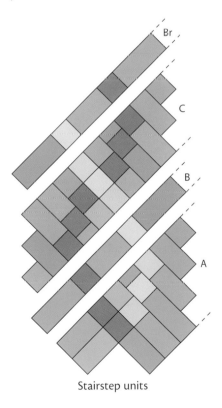

Stairstep units

36. Sew each B unit to its neighboring A, C, or D unit. Then sew the pairs into fours and so on. If this is too confusing, just start with the A unit and keep adding.

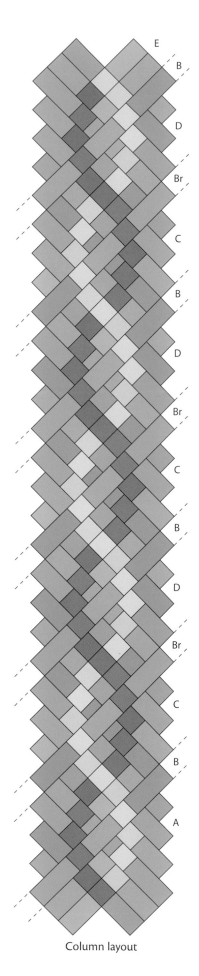

Column layout

37. Construct the lattices by sewing a strip of 1½"-wide outline lattice fabric to each side of a strip of 2½"-wide center lattice fabric. Press the seams toward the center lattice piece.

38. Mark the sides of the pieced columns and trim the ends (pages 12–13).

39. Measure the length of each column to determine the lattice length (pages 13–14). Cut all the lattices to that length. Attach the lattices to 5 of the columns, aligning the lattice edge to the marked line (page 14) and making sure that all columns are oriented in the same direction. Stitch and then trim off the zigzag edges (page 14).

40. Join the units into pairs; then join the pairs.

41. Add the side inner borders first, using the same measurement as the lattice length. Sew and trim them as in Step 39.

42. Add the top and bottom inner borders; then add the outer borders.

43. Layer, quilt, and bind.

Double Helix Stars, 60" × 76"

FRENCH BRAID TRANSFORMATION

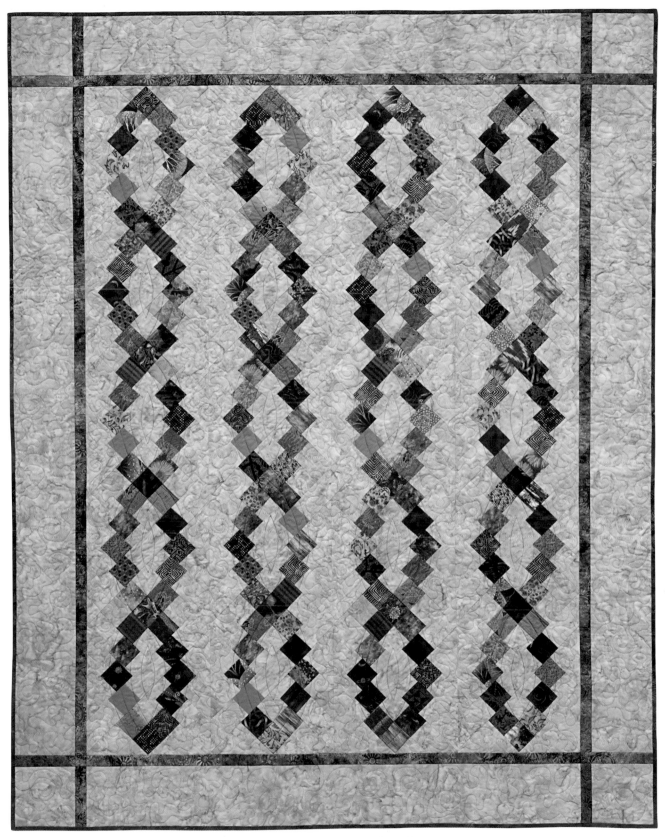

Double Helix Scrappy, 59" × 73"

Although construction is simplified because many units are duplicated, the woven effect is lost.

Lap Double Helix

Double Helix Royal, 54" × 81"

*A*lthough the fabric requirements ask for fat quarters, you can use one nondirectional fabric for all the background pieces. The two accent colors should be similar in value and intensity, and both should contrast with the background. Because the length of the pieced lattices is difficult to adjust, an accurate seam allowance is important.

FABRIC

Background: 15 fat quarters *or* 3⅜ yards of 1 fabric

Colors #1 and #2: 4 fat quarters each

Outline lattice and outer border: 2⅛ yards (2½ yards if directional)

Backing: 5 yards, pieced lengthwise

Binding: ¾ yard

Batting: 58″ × 85″

CUTTING

Background from fat quarters

All strips are width of fat quarter (20″+).

You need a total of 4 strips 7″, 6 strips 5½″, 15 strips 4½″, 5 strips 3½″, 8 strips 2¾″, 16 strips 2½″, and 6 strips 1½″. Group and label the various sizes.

◆ From each of 6 fat quarters, cut 1 strip 5½″, 1 strip 4½″, 1 strip 2½″, and 1 strip 1½″; remove 3 fabrics and cut 1 strip 2¾″ from the remaining 3 fabrics.

◆ From each of 5 fat quarters, cut 1 strip 4½″, 1 strip 3½″, 1 strip 2¾″, and 1 strip 2½″; remove 4 fabrics and cut 1 strip 2½″ from the remaining fabric.

◆ From each of 4 fat quarters, cut 1 strip 7″, 1 strip 4½″, and 1 strip 2½″.

or

Background from yardage

All strips are width of fabric (40″+).

◆ Cut 2 strips 7″, 3 strips 5½″, 8 strips 4½″, 2 strips 3½″, 4 strips 2¾″, 8 strips 2½″, and 3 strips 1½″.

Subcut all strips in half at the center, so they measure 20″+ × their respective lengths.

Subcut a 4½″ half-strip down to 3½″.

Colors #1 and #2

You need 18 strips of color #1 and 15 strips of color #2.

◆ Cut 4 strips 2½″ × width of fabric from each, for a total of 16 of each color.

◆ Cut 2 more strips 2½″ of color #1, for a total of 18.

Outline lattices and outer border

◆ Cut 4 strips 1½″ and 4 strips 5½″, all × length of fabric.

If you have used a directional fabric, as in the photo, refer to page 10 for cutting suggestions.

CONSTRUCTION

Background fabric is referred to as BG, color #1 is purple, and color #2 is magenta. Make a note of your colors, and label and set aside each unit as you cut. There are no E, I, K, O, or Q units. Set aside the 7" and 2¾" strips to use in the pieced lattices. Press each seam as you go. Seams may be pressed in either direction except where otherwise noted.

2½" Squares and 4½" Sets

1. Select 6 BG 2½" strips and cut them into 42 squares 2½" × 2½". Label them F.

2. Select 3 BG 4½" strips and 3 color #1 strips. Seam each BG strip to a color #1 strip, matching the long edges. Press toward the larger strip. Subcut 24 segments to 2½". Label them G.

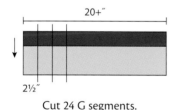

Cut 24 G segments.

3. From a strip of color #1, cut 6 squares 2½" × 2½". Select 6 G segments. Sew a color #1 square to each segment as shown. Press both seams toward the 4½" segment. Label them H.

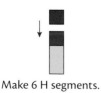

Make 6 H segments.

4. Select 3 BG 4½" strips and 3 color #2 strips. Sew and cut as in Step 2. Label them J.

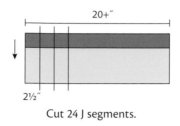

Cut 24 J segments.

5. Select 6 J segments. Sew an F square to the color #2 square on each segment as shown. Press both seams toward the BG square. Label them L.

Make 6 L segments.

6. Subcut the 9 remaining 4½" BG strips into 66 segments 2½". Label them M.

5½" Sets and 3½" Sets

7. Select 3 BG 5½" strips and 3 color #1 strips. Seam each BG strip to a color #1 strip, matching the long edges. Press. Subcut 18 segments to 2½". Label them N.

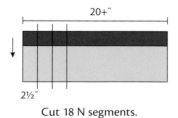

Cut 18 N segments.

8. Select 3 BG 5½" strips and 3 color #2 strips. Sew and cut as in Step 7, using color #2 instead of color #1, and subcutting 24 segments. Label them P.

9. Select 6 P segments. Sew the color #2 end of each segment onto a 1½"

BG strip. Press. Recut the segments to include the 1½" piece. Label them R.

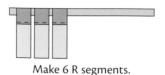

Make 6 R segments.

10. Select 3 BG 3½" strips, 3 BG 1½" strips, and 3 color #1 strips. Sew each color #1 strip between a 3½" and a 1½" BG strip, matching the long edges. Press. Subcut 18 segments to 2½". Label them S.

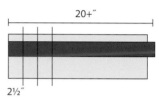

Cut 18 S segments.

11. Select 2 BG 3½" strips, 2 strips 1½" of BG, and 2 color #2 strips. Sew as in Step 10, using color #2 instead of color #1 and subcutting only 12 segments. Label them T.

Nine-Patches

If you want the scrappier look shown, cut the color strips in Steps 12–15 into shorter pieces about 8" long. Mix and match to obtain the desired number of segments. This will take a bit more fabric and time.

12. Select 6 BG 2½" strips and 3 color #1 strips. Sew each color #1 strip between 2 BG strips, matching the long edges. Press seams toward the BG strips. Subcut 18 segments to 2½". Label them U.

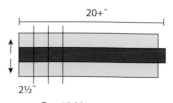

Cut 18 U segments.

13. Select 4 BG 2½" strips and 2 color #2 strips. Sew as in Step 12, using color #2 instead of color #1 and subcutting only 12 segments. Label them V.

14. Select 3 strips of color #1. Sew the long sides together into a set of 3 strips. Press seams toward the center strips. Subcut into 6 segments 2½". Label them W.

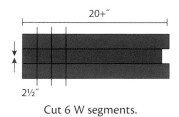

20+"

2½"

Cut 6 W segments.

15. Select 3 strips of color #2. Sew as in Step 14, using color #2 instead of color #1 and subcutting into 8 segments. Label them X. You will need a ninth X segment—make this from 3 squares of color #2.

16. Select 12 M segments. Sew them into 6 pairs, stitching the long edges together. Label them Y.

M   M

Make 6 Y units.

17. Select 36 M segments and 36 F squares. Sew an F square to each M segment, orienting as shown. Label them Z.

M   F

Make 36 Z units.

18. Refer to the King Double Helix instructions for A Units (page 25, Steps 19–23). Use 6 H, 6 L, 6 R, 6 J, 6 Y, and 6 Z units to make 6 A units. *Note: In those instructions, color #1 is orange and color #2 is yellow.*

19. Refer to the King Double Helix instructions for C Units (page 26, Steps 28–31). Use 18 U, 9 X, 18 S, 18 G, and 18 Z units to make 9 C Units.

20. Refer to the King Double Helix instructions for D Units (page 27, Step 32). Use 12 V, 6 W, 12 T, 12 J, and 12 Z units to make 6 D Units.

21. Refer to the King Double Helix instructions for B Units (page 27, Step 33). Use 18 N, 18 M, and 18 P units to make 18 B units.

There are no E units.

Columns

Make 3 columns, each beginning and ending with an A unit. If possible, lay out all 3 columns before you sew.

22. Lay out an A unit so the long straight edge is at a 45° angle. Add a B unit, stairstepping up half the width of the adjacent accent (1"). You can either measure and mark the center of the accent or just estimate.

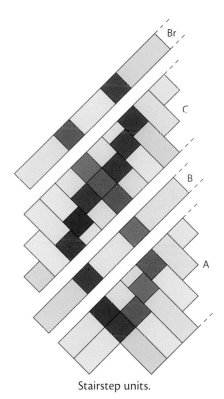

Stairstep units.

23. Add a C unit, stairstepping half of an accent square in the same direction. Turn a B unit 180° (Br) and add it; then add a D unit, stairstepping as before. Continue adding units in the same order (B, C, Br, D) until you have 2 complete sequences. Then add B, C, Br, A to finish the column.

24. Sew each B or Br unit to its neighboring A, C, or D unit. Then sew the pairs into fours and so on. If this is too confusing, just start with an A unit and keep adding.

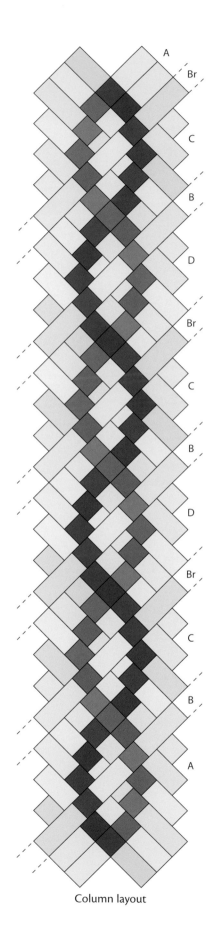

A
Br
C
B
D
Br
C
B
D
Br
C
B
A

Column layout

Pieced Lattices

25. Select 4 BG 2¾" strips and 2 color #2 strips. Sew a 2¾" BG strip to each side of each color #2 strip. Press; subcut 14 segments to 2½".

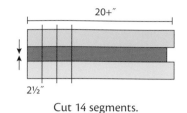

20+"

2½"

Cut 14 segments.

26. Select 4 BG 2¾" strips and 2 color #1 strips. Sew a 2¾" BG strip to each side of each color #1 strip. Press; subcut 12 segments to 2½", as shown in Step 25.

27. Subcut the 7" BG strips into 28 segments 2½".

28. Turn all the 2½" × 7" segments right side up. Measure and mark in the seam allowance 2" from an end on either long edge. Turn the segment 180° and make a similar mark on the other long edge.

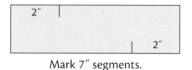

2"

2"

Mark 7" segments.

29. Place the unpieced segment on a flat surface, right side up. Place a pieced segment facedown on top of it. Slide the pieced segment down until its end meets the mark you drew on the unpieced segment. Sew; press the seam toward the unpieced segment.

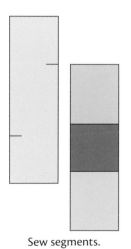

Sew segments.

30. Sew the remaining segments into pairs. Sew 6 pairs with color #1 squares and 7 pairs with color #2 squares into 1 long strip, alternating colors. Begin and end with color #2 and stairstep as in Step 29. Add an unpieced segment after the last pieced segment. Repeat for the second lattice.

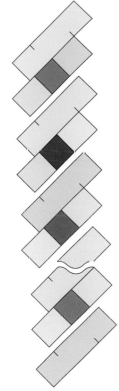

Stairstepped lattice columns

ASSEMBLY

31. Mark the sides of the helix columns and trim the ends (pages 12–13). Use the same method to mark the sides and trim the ends of the lattices, marking them 1 ¾" from their vertical centers.

32. Measure the length of the columns and lattices. If your seam allowances have not been accurate, the difference in length between the helix and lattice columns may be too large to average. In that case, add background pieces to either the helix or the lattice columns, whichever set is shorter. Average the lengths of the unlengthened set of columns and trim the adjusted columns to that length. Cut 4 outline lattices that length.

33. Construct the lattices by sewing a 1½"-wide strip of outline lattice fabric to each side of each pieced lattice (page 14). Trim off the zigzag edges (page 14) and press the seams toward the outline lattice.

34. Attach the lattices to 2 of the columns, aligning the lattice edge to the marked line (page 14). Stitch and then trim off the zigzag edges (page 14).

35. Join these units into a pair; then add the third helix column.

36. Add the side outer borders first, using the same measurement as the lattice length. Sew and trim them as in Step 34.

37. Add the top and bottom outer borders.

38. Layer, quilt, and bind.

The Wave

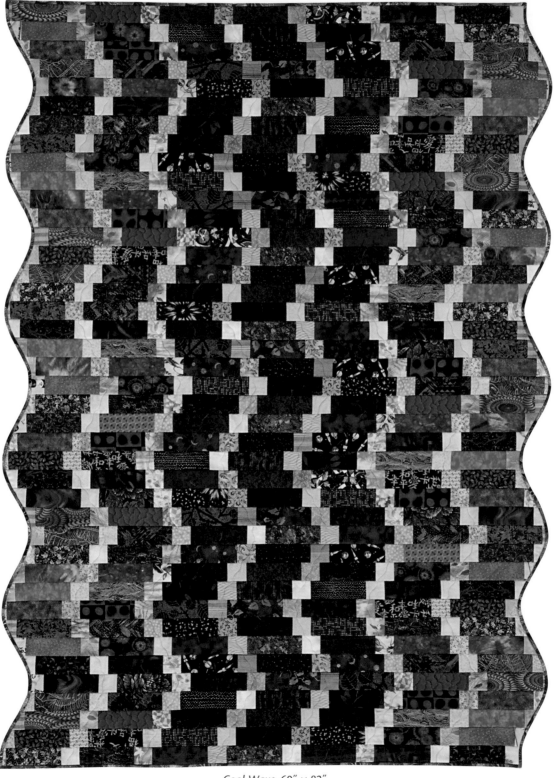

Cool Wave, 60″ × 82″

*P*rints that run parallel to the selvage will be lying on their sides in the finished quilt. You may use smaller pieces of more fabrics if you like, as shown in the photo. Read the fabric requirements and cutting instructions before deciding.

FABRIC

Waves: Fat eighths—6 dark purple, 12 dark blue, 11 dark teal, and 11 dark green

Accents: Fat eighths—12 light purple, 11 light blue, 11 light teal, and 11 light green

or 1⅛ yards (or 7 fat quarters) of 1 accent fabric

Backing: 5 yards, pieced lengthwise
(Read Step 8 before purchasing.)

Binding: ¾ yard

Batting: 64″ × 86″

CUTTING

Waves

◆ Cut 1 strip 6½″ × 20″+ from each fat eight

Accents

◆ From each fat eighth, cut 1 strip 2½″ × 20″+.

or

◆ From yardage, cut 23 strips 2½″ × wof*; subcut each strip into 2 pieces 2½″ × 20″+.

or

◆ From fat quarters of 1 fabric, cut 45 strips 2½″ × width of fat quarter (20″+).

* wof = width of fabric

CONSTRUCTION

When sewing the accent strips to the wave strips, place the accent strip on top. Align the strips at one end of each strip set. Press seams toward the 6½″ strips. There will be extra segments of each color.

1. Sew the long edge of a light purple accent strip to *each* long edge of each dark purple strip. Make 6 sets. Press.

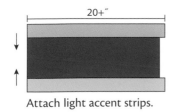

20+″

Attach light accent strips.

2. Sew the long edge of a dark blue strip to the remaining long edge of each light purple accent from Step 1. Press. Subcut each blue/purple strip set into 8 segments 2½″, for a total of about 48. If you fold the set for cutting, make sure that the seams are parallel and that you cut at right angles to the strata.

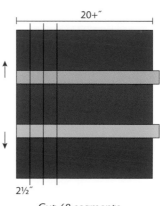

20+″

2½″

Cut 48 segments.

3. Sew the long edge of a light teal accent strip to a long edge of each dark teal strip. Press. Make 11 sets.

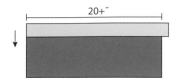

Sew light teal accent to dark teal strip.

4. Sew the long edge of a light blue accent strip to the other long edge of each dark teal strip. Press.

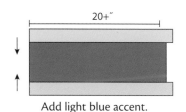

Add light blue accent.

5. Sew the long edge of a light green accent strip to an edge of each dark green strip. Press.

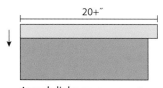

Attach light green accent.

6. Sew the dark green edge of a green strip set to the light teal accent edge of a teal/light blue strip set. Press. Subcut each green/teal strip set into 8 segments 2½", for a total of about 88. If you fold the set for cutting, make sure that the seams are parallel and that you cut at right angles to the strata.

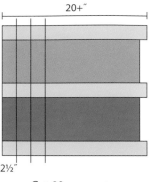

Cut 88 segments.

7. Lay out 41 of the purple/blue segments horizontally, with their long edges adjacent. Arrange them to form 1 large purple and 2 large blue vertical stripes, taking care not to let any fabric abut itself. Rearrange the strips until you are pleased with the progression, remembering that you can turn them 180°. This section will become the 3 center waves.

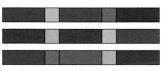

Lay out 41 center sections.

8. Place the light blue accent end of a teal/green segment on each dark blue end of each center purple/blue segment, distributing the prints evenly. If you don't mind that the curve on the edge is incomplete, you may use the leftover pieces to lengthen the quilt by a few rows (about 6").

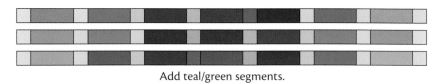

Add teal/green segments.

9. When you are pleased with the arrangement, sew the end of each teal/green segment to its respective center segment. Press.

10. Offset the resulting long strips by 1″ each (half the width of the accent square). You may either mark the center of the accents in the seam allowance or just estimate. Leaving the top strip where it is, work in groups of 4. Slide the first of the next 4 strips to the right 1″. Slide the second strip to the right of the previous strip by 1″. Continue with the third and fourth strips. It's easy to lose your place, so you might want to mark the fourth strip by placing a pin or an office dot on it. For the next group of 4, reverse and slide the first of the 4 strips to the left of the previous by 1″; slide the second, third, and fourth strips 1″ to the left. The fourth strip should align with the top strip. When you start again with another group of 4, place the first strip 1″ to the right of the last strip in the previous group. Slide each of the remaining 3 strips 1″ to the right. Continue in groups of 4 until you have the original strip at the top plus 10 groups of 4.

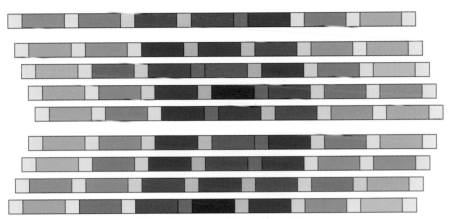

Work in groups of 4 to offset strips.

11. Sew the strips together into pairs, fours, and so on, pinning at the accent squares. To avoid making the quilt into a giant arc, always sew with either the odd- or even-numbered strips on top. Press all seams in the same direction.

FINISHING

12. Layer and quilt.

13. Use the template (page 41) to mark the stairstepped edges in a continuous, pleasing curve. You may need to adjust the curve slightly to allow for shrinkage during quilting. Staystitch about ⅛″ inside the line.

14. Trim on the line and bind, using bias binding on the curved edges.

Green Wave, 76″ × 94″

The Wave was enlarged by completing each strip with 1½″, 2½″, 3½″, or 4½″ pieces and adding borders.

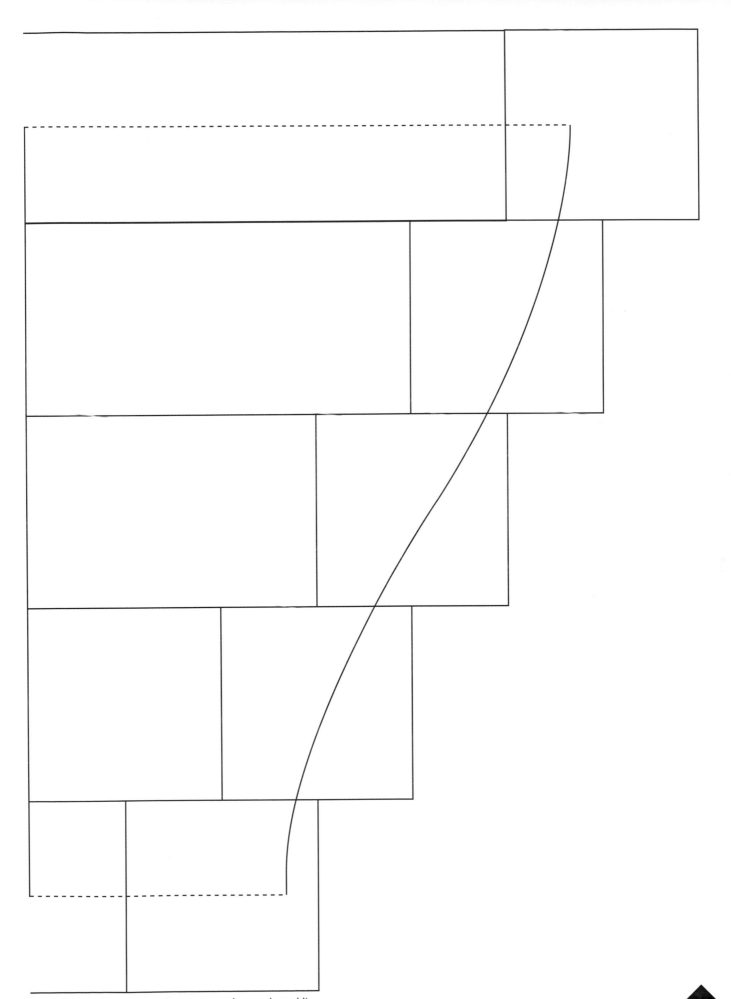

Mark and trim on curve. Reverse template at dotted lines.

The Wavelet

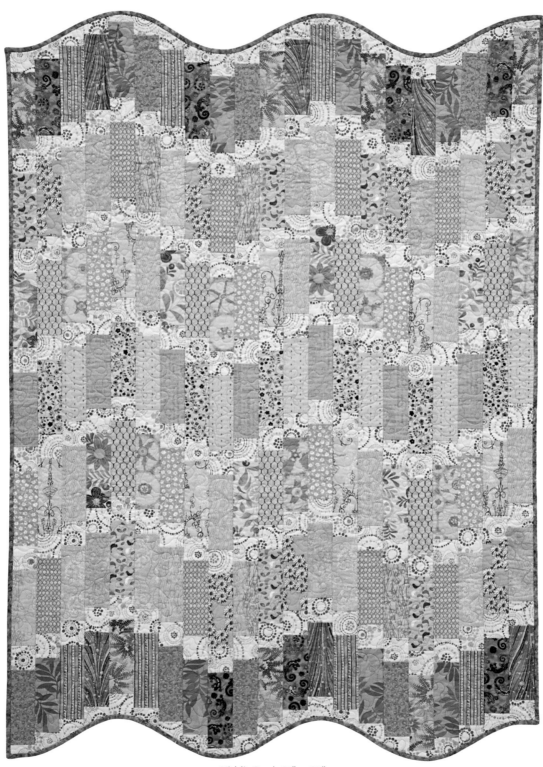

Kiddie Pool, 42" × 60"

*T*his project is half of The Wave turned 90°.

FABRIC

Waves: Fat eighths—9 green, 6 yellow, and 6 turquoise

Accent: 1 yard *or* 4 fat quarters

Backing: 2¾ yards, pieced crosswise (Read Step 6 before buying.)

Binding: ⅝ yard

Batting: 46″ × 64″

CUTTING

Waves

◆ Cut 1 strip 6½″ × 20″+ from each fat eight.

Accent

◆ From yardage, cut 12 strips 2½″ × wof*.

   Subcut each strip into 2 pieces 2½″ × 20″+.

   or

◆ From fat quarters, cut 24 strips 2½″ × width of fat quarter (20″+).

* *wof = width of fabric*

CONSTRUCTION

When sewing the accent strips to the wave strips, place the accent strip on top. Align the strips at one end of each strip set. Press seams toward the 6½″ strips. There will be extra segments of each color.

1. Sew the long edge of an accent strip to *each* long edge of each green strip. Press.

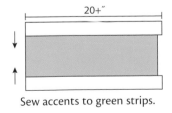

Sew accents to green strips.

2. Set aside 6 of the accented green strip sets to use in Step 4. The remaining 3 accented green strip sets will be the center wave; sew a yellow strip to the accent strip on each side of each of the 3 green strip sets selected. Press. Subcut each of the 3 yellow/green strip sets into 8 segments 2½″, for a total of about 24. If you fold the set for cutting, make sure that the seams are parallel and that you cut at right angles to the strata.

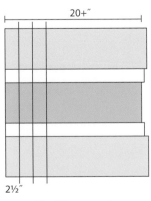

Cut 24 segments.

3. Sew the long edge of an accent strip to 1 long edge of each turquoise strip. Press.

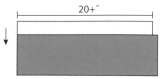

Sew accents to turquoise strips.

4. Sew the long turquoise edge of a strip from Step 3 to a long edge of each remaining accent/green strip set from Step 1. Press. Subcut each green/turquoise strip set into 8 pieces 2½", for a total of about 48 pieces. If you fold the set for cutting, make sure that the seams are parallel and that you cut at right angles to the strata.

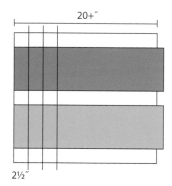

Cut 48 segments.

5. Lay out 21 of the green/yellow segments with their long edges adjacent. Arrange them to form 1 large green and 2 large yellow stripes, taking care not to let any fabric abut itself. Rearrange the strips until you are pleased with the progression, remembering that you can turn them 180°. This section will become the 3 center waves.

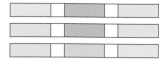

Arrange 21 center segments.

6. Place the accent/green end of a green/turquoise segment on each yellow end of each center strip, distributing the prints evenly. If you don't mind that the curves on the ends are incomplete, you may use the leftover pieces to widen the quilt by a few rows (about 6").

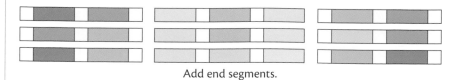

Add end segments.

7. When you are pleased with the arrangement, sew the end of each turquoise/green strip to its respective center strip. Press.

FINISHING

8. Follow the instructions for The Wave (page 39), Steps 10–14, to offset the strips and finish the quilt.

ZigZag, 42" × 68"

This variation was made by offsetting the rows by a full accent, rather than by half; finishing the strips with 2½" and 4½" pieces; and adding a border.

Stax

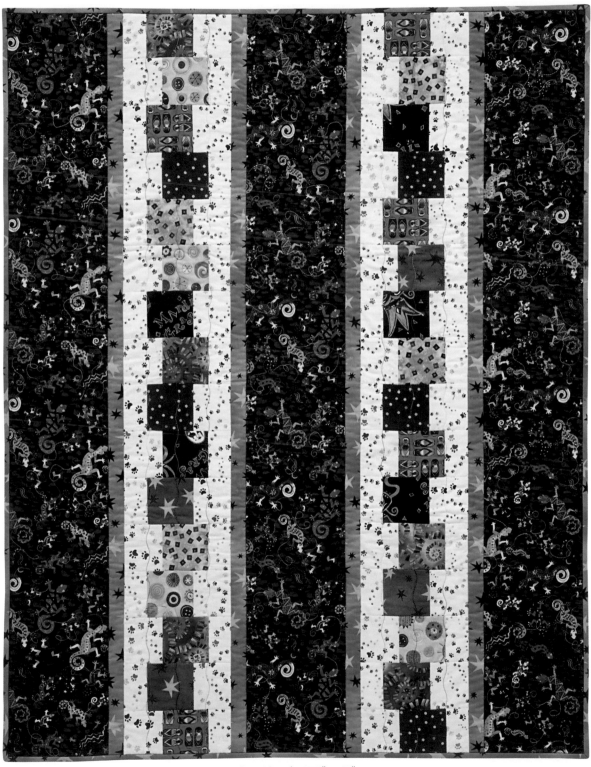

Stax Lizards, 37½" × 48"

*T*his has become my favorite gift quilt. It's fast and fun, uses up odd pieces of fabric, and is easily adaptable to any colors or theme, including a favorite team or school. It works well with or without borders, and the crib size can double as a wallhanging.

FABRIC SELECTION

Pick the main print for the wide columns first; then select scraps or fat eighths for the stacked squares. Choose fabric(s) for the background of the pieced columns and the lattices last. Prints that run parallel to the selvage will be lying on their sides in the pieced columns. You can use fewer fabrics for the squares, as long as you have enough for the total number needed; however, the quilt will not be as scrappy.

FABRIC

Quilt size (w × l)	Main print / Wide columns	Light print / Background pieced columns		Stacked squares: fat eighths or large scraps	Lattice	Borders	Backing	Binding
		If fat quarters (FQs)	If yardage					
CRIB (37½" × 48")	1½ yards	3 FQs	¾ yard	7	⅓ yard	None	1½ yards	½ yard
LAP (46½"– 55½" × 72")	2¼ yards	4 FQs	⅞ yard	10	½ yard	None	3⅜ yards (x/w) 4¼ yards (l/w)	⅝ yard
TWIN (58½"– 67½" × 90")	2⅜ yards	4 FQs	1 yard	11	½ yard	INNER ½ yard OUTER 1½ yards	5¼ yards (l/w)	¾ yard
QUEEN (91" × 96")	5⅝ yards	9 FQs	2 yards	26	1 yard	None	8½ yards (l/w)	⅞ yard
KING (105" × 95")	4¾ yards	8 FQs	1¾ yards	22	⅞ yard	INNER ½ yard OUTER 2 yards	8½ yards (l/w)	⅞ yard

CUTTING

Quilt size / Number of columns	Main print (cut lengthwise)	Light print / Background pieced columns		Stacked squares: cut/configuration	Lattice	Borders
		If fat quarters	If yardage			
CRIB 2 pieced + 3 unpieced	3 strips 7″ × lof*	7 strips 2″ × wof** 7 strips 3″ × wof	4 strips 2″ × wof** 4 strips 3″ × wof	1 strip 3½″ × 18″+ of each / 2 columns, 16 squares each	5 strips 1½″ × wof**	None
LAP 2 pieced + 3 unpieced	3 strips 10″– 13″ × lof	10 strips 2″ × wof 10 strips 3″ × wof	5 strips 2″ × wof 5 strips 3″ × wof	1 strip 3½″ × 18″+ of each / 2 columns, 24 squares each	8 strips 1½″ × wof	None
TWIN 2 pieced + 3 unpieced	3 strips 10″– 13″ × lof	11 strips 2″ × wof 11 strips 3″ × wof	6 strips 2″ × wof 6 strips 3″ × wof	1 strip 3½″ × 18″+ of each / 2 columns, 26 squares each	8 strips 1½″ × wof	INNER 7 strips 1½″ × wof OUTER 8 strips 5½″ × wof
QUEEN 4 pieced + 5 unpieced	Cut fabric in half crosswise; then cut 5 strips 11½″ × lof	26 strips 2″ × wof 26 strips 3″ × wof	13 strips 2″ × wof 13 strips 3″ × wof	1 strip 3½″ × 18″+ of each / 4 columns, 32 squares each	20 strips 1½″ × wof	None
KING 4 pieced + 5 unpieced	Cut fabric in half crosswise; then cut 5 strips 11½″ × lof	22 strips 2″ × wof 22 strips 3″ × wof	11 strips 2″ × wof 11 strips 3″ × wof	1 strip 3½″ × 18″+ of each / 4 columns, 27 squares each	17 strips 1½″ × wof	INNER 9 strips 1½″ × wof OUTER 10 strips 6½″ × wof

* lof = length of fabric

** wof = width of fabric

CONSTRUCTION

If you have cut the background from yardage, first cut each strip in half to obtain 2 pieces 3″ × 20″+ or 2 pieces 2″ × 20″+.

1. Sew a 3″ background strip to a long edge of each 3½″ stacked-square strip. Press the seam toward the darker fabric.

2. Sew a 2″ background strip to the other long edge of each stacked-square strip. Press the seam toward the darker fabric.

3. Subcut into 3½″ segments. You will obtain 5 segments from each strip.

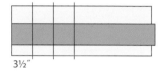

3½″

4. Refer to the chart (page 47) to determine the number of columns and the number of segments in each. Piece the segments into pairs, reversing every other segment so that the colored squares are staggered. You may sew the segments in random order or repeat them in the same order. Either way, keep the orientation of the 2 segments the same from pair to pair.

Stagger segment pairs.

5. Refer to the chart (page 47) to determine the number of pieced columns. Sew the segment pairs into columns. (Add an extra segment to each column for the king size.) Press all the seams in the same direction.

ASSEMBLY

6. Piece the lattice strips end to end to make 1 long piece.

7. Measure the lengths of the pieced columns down the center. If the lengths are all the same, use that number. If they are different, average them and use that number rounded up to the nearest ¼″.

8. You need 2 lattices for each pieced column. Cut them the length determined in Step 7.

9. Match the center, ends, and quarters of each pieced column to the center, ends, and quarters of a lattice strip. Sew. Repeat for the other edge of each pieced column. Press the seams toward the lattices.

10. Refer to the chart (page 47) to determine the number and width of unpieced columns to cut, or use a width you prefer. Cut the required number, using the length from Step 7 for your cut length.

11. Sew the lattice to the edge of an unpieced column, matching the ends and centers. Repeat for all the pieced columns. If your unpieced column fabric is directional, be sure to check the orientation before sewing. Then sew the pairs together into a top.

12. Add a border, if desired.

13. Layer, quilt, and bind.

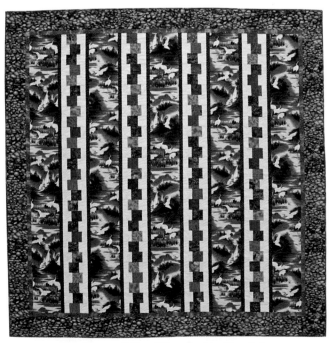

Stax Cranes, 90″ × 95″, quilted by Lisa Calle

Stax Muscle, 61″ × 93″

Stax Sassaman, 48½" × 72"

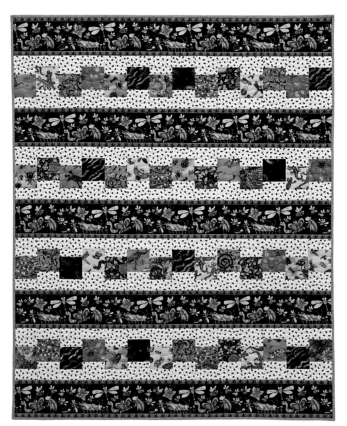

Stax Bugs, 42" × 58"

The pattern will also work in a horizontal configuration.

Erector Set

Erector Set Brights, 60" × 76"

*A*lthough this quilt looks as if there must be a Y-seam somewhere, it's actually made up of large triangles sewn into six straight columns. The dots reminded me of rivets; hence the name.

FABRIC

Zigzag: Fat quarters (not straight quarters)—7 dark and 7 light

Dots: Several fat eighths or scraps for dots (⅝ yard if using 1 fabric)

Fusible web: 1¼ yards (if used for appliqué)

Inner border: ⅜ yard

Outer border: 2 yards cut lengthwise *or* 1¼ yards cut crosswise

Backing: 3¾ yards pieced crosswise *or* 4⅝ yards pieced lengthwise

Binding: ¾ yard

Batting: 64″ × 80″

CUTTING

Fat quarters

Divide the dark fat quarters into a set of 4 fat quarters and another set of 3 fat quarters. The fabrics in the set of 3 will appear at the ends of the columns and less frequently within the columns.

◆ From each fabric in the set of 4, cut 1 square 17¼″.

Subcut each square twice diagonally to obtain 16 quarter-square triangles.

◆ From each fabric in the set of 3, first cut 1 square 8⅞″ from a corner, being careful not to extend the cuts into the center of the fat quarters.

Subcut these squares once diagonally to obtain 6 half-square triangles. Then cut 2 quarter-square triangles from the opposite corner, each with a 17¼″ base, to obtain 6.

Divide the 7 light fat quarters into sets as was done for the darks and cut in the same way.

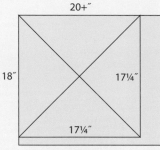

Cut 4 like this.

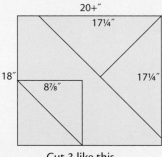

Cut 3 like this.

Dots

◆ Cut 27 dots 4″–5″ in diameter. See Adding the Dots (page 54) to determine size.

Inner border

◆ Cut 6 strips 1½″ × wof*.

Outer border

◆ Cut 4 strips 5½″ × length of fabric *or* 7 strips 5½″ × wof.

* wof = width of fabric

CONSTRUCTION

1. Refer to the illustration for Steps 4 and 5 as you lay out all 6 columns; be sure to distribute the fabrics evenly. Each column consists of 4 large triangles of one color, plus 3 large and 2 small triangles of the other color. There will be 1 large triangle of each color left over.

2. Seam pairs of the large light triangles to adjoining large dark triangles on the shorter sides. To match the point of the 90° angle of one triangle with the point of the 45° angle of the other, slide the 90° angle down ⅜" as shown; then sew the ¼" seam. This may seem wrong, but if you align the triangles differently, their points will be cut off in the finished top.

Seam large triangles.

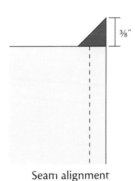

Seam alignment

3. Sew 3 pairs of triangles into a column. Add a large triangle to one end of the column. There will be 2 types of columns—3 that end with dark triangles and 3 that end with light. Press all the seams in the column in the same direction.

4. Add a small triangle to each end of the column, matching the 45° angles. The triangles on both ends of the column will be the same color (either dark or light). Press the seams in the same direction as the others in the column. Repeat Steps 2–4 to construct 5 more columns.

Make 3 columns and 3 with colors reversed.

Add small triangles.

5. Select a column that ends with dark triangles and another column that ends with light triangles. Find the center of the base of each large triangle by folding its base in half. Mark the center with a pin or a pencil line. Match the end of a dark column to the end of a light column; pin the point of each large triangle to the center of the base of the triangle in the adjoining column. Sew the columns together. Repeat for the other 4 columns, orienting the 2 columns the same way in each pair and making sure not to reverse any of them.

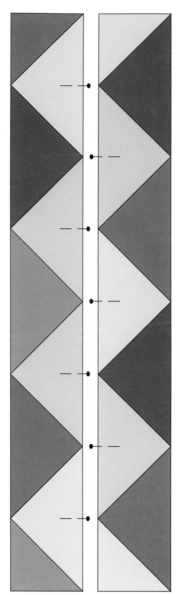

Make 3 sets.

Adding the Dots

Lay out the column pairs as they will appear in the quilt. You will see 3 vertical zigzags of one color and 2 of another. The dots will be placed on the "points" of the 3-zigzag color. The dots on *Erector Set Brights* finish 4½"; the dots on *Erector Set Purple* (page 55) finish 4". You can either make yours a size used here or use a different size or shape entirely. If in doubt, cut dots from paper and place them on the quilt top to decide on the size.

6. Decide how you wish to add the dots: by hand or machine, fused or not. If you use fusible web, follow the manufacturer's instructions to apply it. Cut 27 dots. Place the dots on the points of the 3-zigzag color. Rearrange them until you are happy with the result, positioning them with the outermost dot edges ⅝" from the 2 nearest seams. Place the dots on the ending triangles ⅝" from the outermost diagonal seam, with the *diameter* of the dot on the *seamline* (not on the raw edge) at the end of the column.

Dot placement

7. If you don't want the dots to overlap into the border, cut off the sections that extend past the column ends. Fuse or sew the dots. If you have decided to let the dots overlap into the border, attach only the innermost third of the 6 dots that will adjoin the border.

Attach here.

Attach only one-third of border dots.

ASSEMBLY

8. Sew the 3 column pairs together as in Step 5. Fold back any unattached parts of the dots and pin them to the columns.

9. Attach the inner and outer borders. Unpin and attach any loose dot edges.

10. Layer, quilt, and bind.

Erector Set Purple, 60" × 76"

Quick Celtic Not

Quick Celtic Not—Green, 62½" × 85"

*T*his quilt is made from three columns, each 13"–13½" × 71", and two lattices, each 4", plus borders. Prints will appear on the diagonal in the finished columns, and fabrics with obvious one-way designs will not work well as a background. Colors #1 and #2 must be similar in value and intensity, and both should contrast with the background.

FABRIC

Background: 2¾ yards

Colors #1 and #2: ¾ yard each

Outline lattice, inner border, and optional binding: 1¼ yards

Center lattice and outer border: 2¼ yards, cut lengthwise

Binding: ¾ yard (if different from lattice and inner border)

Backing: 5⅛ yards

Batting: 67" × 89"

CUTTING

Cut from selvage to selvage unless otherwise stated. All strips are at least 40" in length.

Background

◆ Cut 1 strip 10½", 6 strips 8½", and 7 strips 4½".

Subcut the 10½" strip into 6 pieces 4½" × 10½" and 2 pieces 2½" × 10½"; then subcut each 2½" × 10½" piece into 3 pieces 2½" × 3½".

Colors #1 and #2

◆ Cut 1 strip 14½" and 3 strips 2½" from each color.

Outline lattice and inner border

◆ Cut 13 strips 1½" × *length* of fabric. You will have enough fabric left for binding.

Center lattice and outer border

◆ Cut 4 strips 6½" and 2 strips 2½", all × *length* of fabric.

CONSTRUCTION

You need 5 types of units—A, B, C, D, and E; label them as you go. Align strips at one end to sew. Background is referred to as BG, color #1 is pink, and color #2 is blue.

B Units

1. Make 3 sets. Sew a 2½" color #1 strip to a 4½" BG strip. Sew a 2½" color #2 strip to the remaining raw edge of the 4½" BG strip. Press seams toward the 2½" strips. Sew an 8½" BG strip to the remaining raw edge of color #1. Sew another 8½" BG strip to the remaining raw edge of color #2. Press seams toward the 8½" strips. Subcut into 24 segments 4½". If you fold the set for cutting, make sure that the seams are parallel and that you cut at right angles to the strata.

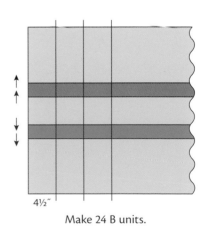

4½"

Make 24 B units.

C Units

2. Sew a 4½" BG strip to each side of the 14½" color #2 strip. Press seams toward the center. Subcut into 12 segments 2½". If you fold the set for cutting, make sure the seams are parallel and that you cut at right angles to the strata.

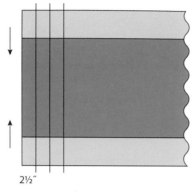

2½"

Make 12 C units.

D Units

3. Sew a 4½" BG strip to the 14½" color #1 strip. Press the seam toward color #1. Subcut a 16" piece from one end and set it aside to use in Step 4.

From another 4½" BG strip, cut a 16" piece; set it aside to use in Step 4.

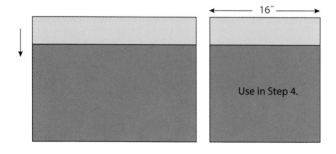

16"

Use in Step 4.

Sew the remaining piece of the cut 4½" BG strip to the remaining raw edge of the larger piece of color #1. Subcut into 9 segments 2½". If you fold the set for cutting, make sure the seams are parallel and that you cut at right angles to the strata.

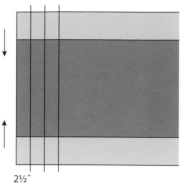

2½"

Make 9 D units.

A Units

4. Cut off and discard a 6" strip from the color #1 edge of the 16" piece of color #1 + BG that you set aside in Step 3. You should have 8¼" from the seam to the new raw edge of color #1. Sew the 16" piece of the 4½" BG strip to this new raw edge. Press the seam toward color #1. Subcut into 6 segments 2½". If you fold the set to subcut, make sure the seams are parallel and that you cut at right angles to the strata.

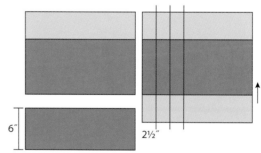

6"

2½"

Make 6 A units.

E Units

5. Sew the long edge of a 2½" × 3½" BG piece to the long edge of a 4½" × 10½" BG piece, matching the centers. Press the seam toward the 3½" piece. Make 6.

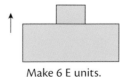

Make 6 E units.

SEWING COLUMNS

Pay close attention to the orientation of each unit and label the sets as you construct them. Read Steps 6–15. If this method is confusing, just start with an A/E unit and add units, referring to the illustration on page 60. Press all seams in Steps 7–14 away from the B and Br units.

6. Sew an E unit to each A unit, placing the raw edge of the E unit ¼" past the seamline in the A unit. Orient the units as shown. Press toward the E unit. Label them Step 6.

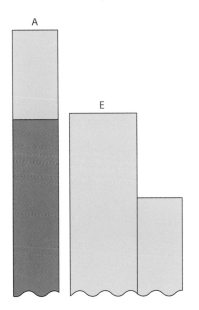

7. Sew each C unit to a B unit, matching seams and orienting as shown. You will have 12 B/C units. Label them Step 7.

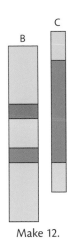

Make 12.

8. Turn the remaining 12 B units 180° to make Br units. Sew each D unit to a Br unit, matching seams and orienting as shown. You will have 9 Br/D units. Label them Step 8.

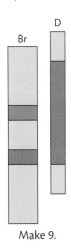

Make 9.

9. Sew a Step 6 unit to each of the 3 remaining Br units, matching seams and orienting as shown. Label them Step 9. You will have 3 Step 6 units left.

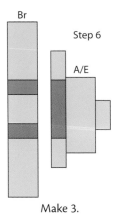

Make 3.

10. Sew each Step 8 unit to a Step 7 unit, orienting and matching as shown. To align the color #1 seams in the B and Br units, first match the long edges of the Br and C units, right sides together. Then match the bottom Br seam to the corresponding seam on the B unit beneath it. You should be able to feel it, even though the B unit seam does not extend all the way to the Br edge. If this method doesn't work well for you, place a ruler on the B seamline so that it extends across the C unit. Make a mark in the C unit's seam allowance and match the seamline in the Br unit to it. The edges of the finished unit should stairstep. Make 9 Step 7 / Step 8 units. Label them Step 10.

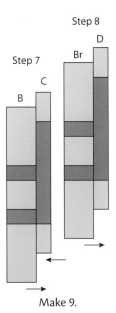

Make 9.

11. Sew each Step 9 unit to a remaining Step 7 unit, matching seams and orienting as shown. Label them Step 11.

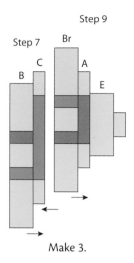

Step 7 Step 9

B C Br A E

Make 3.

12. Sew 6 of the Step 10 units into 3 pairs, matching the seams as in Step 10. Label the units Step 12.

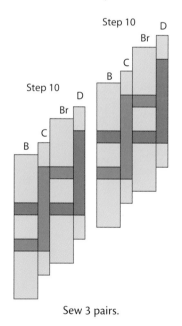

Step 10 D

Step 10 D Br C B

B C Br

Sew 3 pairs.

13. Sew each of the remaining 3 Step 10 units to a Step 11 unit as shown, matching the seams as in Step 10. Label the units Step 13.

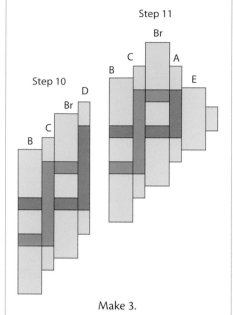

Step 11

Step 10 Br C B A E D

B

Make 3.

14. Follow the illustration to sew a Step 12 unit to a Step 13 unit. Make 2 more columns.

15. Sew a Step 6 unit to the other end of each column, orienting as shown.

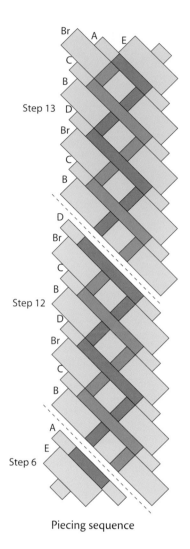

Step 13

Step 12

Step 6

Br A E C B D Br C B D Br C B D Br C B A E

Piecing sequence

ASSEMBLY

16. Sew 2 strips of 1½" outline / inner border fabric end to end to yield 1 or 2 long strips. Cut off as needed.

17. Construct the lattices by sewing a long strip of outline lattice to each side of each 2½" strip of center lattice.

18. Mark the sides of the pieced columns and trim the ends (pages 12–13).

19. Measure the lengths of the columns to determine the lattice length (page 14). Cut both lattices to that length. Attach the lattices to 2 of the columns, aligning the lattice edge to the marked line (page 14). Stitch and then trim off the zigzag edges (page 14).

20. Join these units into a pair; then add the third pieced column.

21. Attach the side inner borders first, using the same measurement as the lattice length. Sew them as in Step 19.

22. Add the top and bottom inner borders; then add the outer borders.

23. Layer, quilt, and bind.

Quick Celtic Not—Laurel, 64" × 83", quilted by Patricia E. Ritter
Pieced lattices add interest.

Quick Celtic Not—Brown, 62½" × 85"

Scrappy Celtic Not

Celtic Not Wedding Quilt, 108" × 104½"

*I*f you prefer to cut from scraps, read the cutting instructions and cut the total number of strips needed. You can obtain a similar effect by cutting as directed from fat quarters.

FABRIC

Background: 29 fat quarters

Colors #1 and #2: 8 fat quarters each

Lattice: 1 yard

Inner border: ⅝ yard

Outer border: 3¼ yards cut lengthwise *or* 2½ yards cut crosswise

Backing: 9½ yards

Binding: 1 yard

Batting: 112" × 109"

CUTTING

Strips for background and colors #1 and #2 are width of fat quarter (20"+).

Background

You need 3 strips 10½", 30 strips 8½", 33 strips 4½", and 3 strips 3½".

◆ From each of 15 fat quarters, cut 2 strips 8½".

◆ From each of 3 fat quarters, cut 1 strip 10½" and 1 strip 4½". Subcut the 10½" strips into 12 pieces 4½" × 10½".

◆ From each of 10 fat quarters, cut 3 strips 4½"; remove 7 fabrics and cut 1 strip 3½" from the remaining 3 fabrics. Subcut the 3½" strips into 12 pieces 2½" × 3½".

If some fat quarters are skimpy, you will have 1 extra fat quarter from which to cut strips. If you have cut from scraps, save background fabric by cutting the E unit pieces for Step 6 from strips that are 21"+.

Color #1

You need 8 strips 4½" and 28 strips 2½".

◆ From each of 4 fat quarters, cut 1 strip 4½" and 4 strips 2½".

◆ From each of 4 fat quarters, cut 1 strip 4½" and 3 strips 2½".

Color #2

You need 8 strips 4½" and 27 strips 2½".

◆ From each of 5 fat quarters, cut 1 strip 4½" and 3 strips 2½".

◆ From each of 3 fat quarters, cut 1 strip 4½" and 4 strips 2½".

Lattice

◆ Cut 12 strips 2½" × wof* (40"+).

Inner borders

◆ Cut 10 strips 1½" × wof* (40"+).

Outer borders

◆ Cut 4 strips 8" × length of fabric *or* cut 10 strips 8" × wof (40"+).

* wof = width of fabric

CONSTRUCTION

You need 5 types of units—A, B, C, D, and E; label them as you go. Background is referred to as BG, color #1 is gold, and color #2 is orange. Remember that the strips referred to are actually half-strips (at least 20" long).

B Units

1. Make 15 sets. Sew an 8½" BG strip to a 2½" color #1 strip; sew a 4½" strip of a different BG to the other edge of the color #1 strip. Sew an 8½" strip of a third BG to a 2½" strip of color #2. Sew the remaining raw edge of the color #2 strip to the remaining raw edge of the 4½" BG strip. Press all seams toward BG. Subcut 60 segments to 4½". If you fold the set for cutting, make sure that the seams are parallel and that you cut at right angles to the strata.

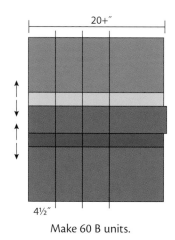

Make 60 B units.

A Units

2. Make 2 sets. Sew the long edge of a 2½" color #1 strip to each long edge of a 4½" color #1 strip, using 3 different color #1 fabrics.

3. Sew a 4½" BG strip to the long edge of each 2½" color #1 strip from Step 2, using 2 different BG fabrics. Press all seams toward the 2½" strips. Subcut 12 segments to 2½". If you fold the set for cutting, make sure that the seams are parallel and that you cut at right angles to the strata.

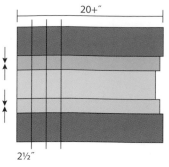

Make 12 A units.

D Units

4. Make 3 sets, using 5 different color #1 fabrics in each set; sew the long edge of a 4½" color #1 strip to each side of a 2½" color #1 strip. Sew a 2½" color #1 strip to each remaining raw edge of the 4½" strips. Sew a 4½" BG strip to each remaining raw edge. Press all seams toward the 2½" strips. Subcut 24 segments to 2½". If you fold the set for cutting, make sure that the seams are parallel and that you cut at right angles to the strata.

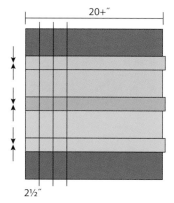

Make 24 D units.

C Units

5. Make 4 sets. Repeat the process in Step 4, substituting color #2 fabrics for color #1. Subcut 30 segments to 2½".

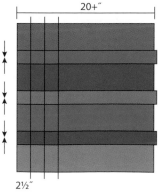

Make 30 C units.

E Units

6. Make 12. Sew the long edge of a 2½″ × 3½″ BG piece to the long edge of each 4½″ × 10½″ BG piece, matching the centers. Press seams toward the 3½″ pieces.

Make 12 E units.

CONSTRUCT COLUMNS

7. If possible, lay out the columns before sewing. Start with an A unit. Add 1 B unit and then 1 C unit, stairstepping each added unit.

8. Turn a B unit 180° to obtain a B reversed (Br) unit and add it to the column, continuing to stairstep. Begin the sequence again, substituting a D unit for the A unit.

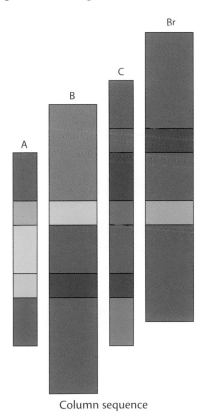

Column sequence

9. Continue adding segments in the order D, B, C, Br until you have 4 complete sets of D, B, C, Br following the first A, B, C, Br set.

10. Add an A unit. There should be 10 diagonal squares in the column.

11. Sew an end unit to each end of each column, extending the raw-edge end of the 10½″ piece ¼″ past the seamline in the A unit. See the illustration for Step 6 (page 59).

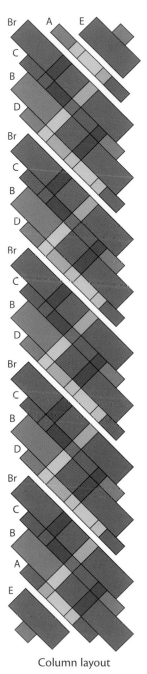

Column layout

12. Make 5 more columns.

ASSEMBLY

13. Sew the lattice strips end to end to yield a long strip.

14. Mark the sides of the pieced columns and trim the ends (pages 12–13).

15. Measure the length of the columns to determine the lattice length (page 14). Cut 5 lattices to that length.

16. Attach the lattices to 5 of the columns, aligning the lattice edges to the marked lines (page 14). Stitch and then trim off the zigzag edges (page 14).

17. Join these units into pairs; then join the pairs.

18. Add the side inner borders first, using the same measurement as for the lattice length. Sew in the same way as for Step 16.

19. Add the top and bottom inner borders; then add the outer borders.

20. Layer, quilt, and bind.

Celtic Not—Blue + Green, 56" × 83", quilted by Patricia E. Ritter

Rat Race

Rat Race Neutrals, 107" × 107", quilted by Patricia E. Ritter

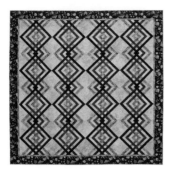

*T*his quilt isn't made in columns, although it looks as if it should be. For the 16½" finished blocks to fit, an accurate seam allowance is necessary.

FABRIC SELECTION

Select a nondirectional background fabric and 6 fabrics for the interwoven lines. The 6 fabrics must have enough contrast with the background to stand out in most places, as well as enough contrast with each other so that the woven effect is maintained. In the photo, color #1 is light gray, color #2 is light brown, color #3 is medium gray, color #4 is medium brown, color #5 is dark gray, and color #6 is dark brown. Make a list of your colors and their respective numbers so that you can keep track of them during cutting and piecing. The quilt can be converted into a queen size (93" × 93") by eliminating the borders.

FABRIC

Background: 6 yards

Colors #1 and #2: 1 yard each

Colors #3, #4, #5, and #6: 1⅛ yards each

Inner border: ⅝ yard

Outer border: 3⅛ yards cut lengthwise *or* 2⅜ yards cut crosswise

Backing: 9½ yards

Binding: 1 yard

Batting: 111" × 111"

CUTTING

All cuts are width of fabric (40"+) unless otherwise stated.

Background
◆ Cut 2 strips 14½", 2 strips 9½", 2 strips 8", 2 strips 6½", 2 strips 5", and 32 strips 2".

You will cut more background after Step 20.

Colors #1 and #2
◆ Cut 14 strips 2" from each.

Colors #3 and #4
◆ Cut 16 strips 2" from each.

Colors #5 and #6
◆ Cut 1 strip 17", 1 strip 14", and 2 strips 2" from each.

Inner border
◆ Cut 10 strips 1½".

Outer border
◆ Cut 4 strips 6½" × length of fabric *or* 11 strips 6½" × wof*.

* *wof = width of fabric*

CONSTRUCTION

Main Blocks

These 16 blocks are built from the center out. The method is similar to Log Cabin or Courthouse Steps blocks. Background is referred to as BG throughout. Pay close attention to the orientation of the block components as you construct them.

1. Sew the long edge of a color #1 strip to the long edge of a 2" BG strip. Sew a color #2 strip to the remaining raw edge of the BG strip. Press seams toward fabrics #1 and #2. Subcut into 16 segments 2".

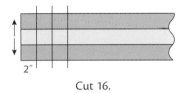

Cut 16.

2. From 3 strips of color #1, cut 16 pieces 6½". Repeat, using 3 strips of color #2. From 3 BG 2" strips, cut 32 pieces, each 3½" long.

3. Sew a 6½" piece of color #1 to each segment from Step 1 as shown, matching the color #1 ends and leaving about half of the seam unsewn. Add a 3½" BG piece to the color #1 end. Add a 6½" piece of color #2 to the side opposite the color #1 piece. Add a 3½" BG piece to the remaining end. Sew the rest of the original seam. Press all seams toward the block's outer edges.

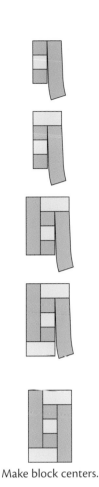

Make block centers.

4. Sew the long edge of a color #1 strip to the long edge of a 2" BG strip. Sew the remaining long edge of color #1 to a 5" BG strip. Press seams toward the darker fabric. Repeat, substituting color #2 for color #1. Subcut each piece into 16 segments 2".

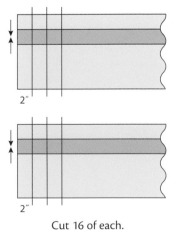

Cut 16 of each.

5. Sew a color #1 segment from Step 4 to the color #2 side of each block center, matching the seamlines to the color #1 seamlines in the block's center. For the best accuracy, place a ruler along the original seamlines and mark the outer edge of the block in the seam allowance. Then match the seamlines of the new piece to the marks. Repeat on the color #1 side of the block, using a color #2 segment from Step 4. Press whichever way the seam wants to fall, probably toward the block's center.

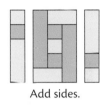

Add sides.

6. From 4 strips of color #3, cut 16 pieces 8". Repeat with color #4. Sew the strips onto the ends of your block, orienting as shown. Do not sew the pieces to the sides you added in Step 5.

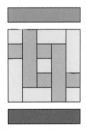

Add top and bottom.

7. Sew together the long edges of a 2" BG strip and a color #1 strip. Repeat with another BG strip and color #3. Sew the long BG edge of the color #1 + BG piece to the color #3 edge of the color #3 + BG piece. Sew a 6½" BG strip to the remaining long raw edge of color #1. Press seams toward the darker fabrics. Subcut into 16 segments 2".

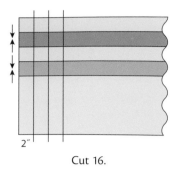

Cut 16.

8. Repeat Step 7 with colors #2 and #4. Press seams toward the darker fabrics. Subcut into 16 segments 2″.

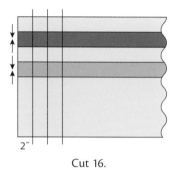

Cut 16.

9. From 6 strips of color #3, cut 16 pieces 12½″. Sew 1 piece to each BG + #2 + #4 piece from Step 8. Repeat, substituting color #4 for color #3 and the BG + #1 + #3 pieces from Step 7. Orient the pieces as shown. Press seams toward the unpieced segments.

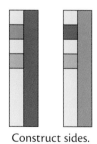

Construct sides.

10. Sew together the long edges of a color #1 strip and a 2″ BG strip. Sew an 8″ BG strip to the other long edge of color #1. Repeat, substituting color #2 for color #1. Press seams toward the darker fabrics and subcut each piece into 16 segments 2″.

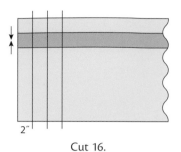

Cut 16.

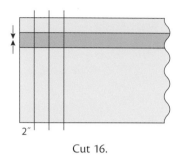

Cut 16.

11. Add the segments from Steps 9 and 10 to the block, using the same method as in Step 3. Orient the block as shown in the illustration.

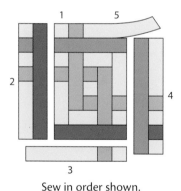

Sew in order shown.

12. Subcut each of the 14″ and 17″ strips of fabrics #5 and #6 into 16 segments 2″. Orient the blocks as shown and sew a 14″ piece of color #5 to one side of each block; then sew a 14″ piece of color #6 to the opposite side. Press seams toward the outer edges. Sew a 17″ piece of each fabric to the remaining sides, orienting as shown. Press seams toward the outer edges.

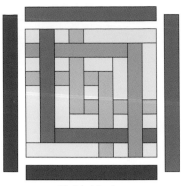

Finish blocks.

Alternating Blocks and Side Setting Triangles

Make 12 units from colors #5, #3, and #1 and 12 units from colors #6, #4, and #2. Instructions are for the 5-3-1 units.

13. Sew together the long edges of a 2″ strip of color #5 and a 2″ BG strip. Press the seam toward BG and subcut into 12 segments 2″.

14. Sew a long edge of each of 3 color #3 strips to the long edge of each of 3 BG 2″ strips. Press the seams toward the darker fabric. Subcut 12 segments 3½″ and 12 segments 5″.

15. Sew the BG edge of a 3½″ piece of color #3 + BG from Step 14 to the longer side of each color #5 + BG segment from Step 13, orienting as shown. Press seams toward the 3½″ piece.

16. Sew the color #3 edge of a 5″ piece of color #3 + BG from Step 14 to the longer side of each color #5 + BG rectangle from Step 15, orienting as shown. Press seams toward the 5″ piece.

17. Sew a long edge of each of 2 color #1 strips to the long edge of each of 2 BG 2″ strips. Press the seams toward the darker fabric. Subcut 12 segments 6½″.

18. Sew the BG edge of a 6½″ piece of the color #1 + BG strip from Step 17 to the longer side of each color #5 + color #3 + BG rectangle from Step 16, orienting as shown. Press seams toward the 6½″ piece.

19. From 3 strips of color #1, cut 12 pieces 8″. Sew a piece to the BG edge of each color 5-3-1 rectangle from Step 18. Press seams toward the 8″ piece.

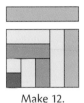

Make 12.

20. Repeat Steps 13–19, substituting color #6 for color #5, color #4 for color #3, and color #2 for color #1.

Make 12.

Decision Time

You now have 16 main blocks and 24 corners for the alternating blocks and side setting triangles. It's time to decide on their eventual arrangement.

The quilt is set on-point, with the main blocks set 4 × 4. Lay them out and decide whether you like colors #5, #3, and #1 or colors #6, #4, and #2 pointing toward the center. If you decide that colors #5, #3, and #1 in the main blocks nearest the center of the quilt will point toward the center, then the 3 center alternating blocks and the 6 side setting triangles will consist of colors #6, #4, and #2, and the 6 side alternating blocks will be made of colors #5, #3, and #1. The main blocks in the side rows must be mirror images of their adjoining center main blocks. The following instructions assume that this is the case. If you orient the center main blocks differently, adjust the instructions accordingly.

Alternating Blocks

There are two ways to piece these 9 blocks. The first method (Steps 21–24) uses long, straight seams that run across the center of the alternating center blocks. The second method (Steps 26–30) uses Y-seams, but minimizes the number of seams in the center of the quilt. Read both sets of instructions and decide which you will use before cutting the remaining background pieces. Make 3 blocks from colors #6, #4, and #2 for the center columns and 6 blocks from colors #5, #3, and #1 for the side columns. You will have 6 leftover 6-4-2 corners, which will be used later.

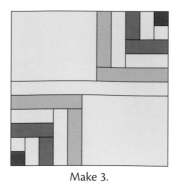

Make 3.

Method 1—More Seams, Easier Construction

21. Cut 5 strips 2" and 5 strips 8" of BG, all × width of fabric. From the 2" strips, cut 9 pieces 17". From the 8" strips, cut 18 rectangles 8" × 9½".

22. Sew a color #2 edge of 6 of the 6-4-2 units from Step 20 to the 8" side of an 8" × 9½" BG rectangle, orienting as shown. Press seams toward the rectangles.

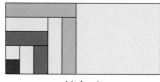

Make 6.

23. Sew a 2" × 17" BG rectangle to the remaining color #2 side of 3 of the rectangles from Step 22, orienting as shown. Press seams toward the 17" piece.

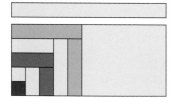

24. Sew the rectangle from Step 23 to each remaining rectangle from Step 22, orienting as shown. Press toward the center.

25. Use the remaining pieces from Step 21 and the twelve 5-3-1 blocks from Step 19 to make 6 more blocks.

Method 2—Fewer Seams, More Complicated Construction

26. From BG, cut 5 strips 9½" × width of fabric. Subcut 18 squares 9½" × 9½".

27. Sew a color #2 edge of each of 6 pieced 6-4-2 squares from Step 20 to a 9½" BG square, orienting and matching as shown and ending the seam at the seamline in the color #2 corner of the pieced square. Press seams toward BG.

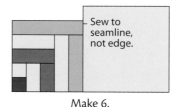

Make 6.

28. Place a pair of "rectangles" from Step 27 right sides together and sew each remaining color #2 edge to the BG rectangles as shown. End the seam at the "center" seamline. There will be a hole in the center of the block. Press seams toward BG.

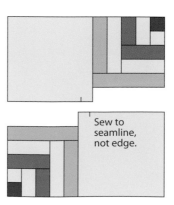

29. Fold each block diagonally, with the corners of the BG rectangles together and the sides aligned. Pull out the center corners; fold up and pin the pressed seams so that they are out of the way at the center of the block.

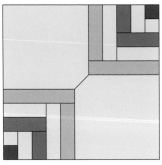

Make 3.

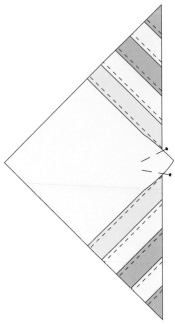

Pin seam allowances out of the way.

31. Use the remaining pieces from Step 26 and the twelve 5-3-1 blocks from Step 19 to make 6 more blocks.

Side Setting Triangles

32. From 2 BG 14½" strips, cut 4 squares 14½". Subcut twice diagonally to yield 16 quarter-square triangles. Set aside and label 4 triangles to use in Step 46.

33. Sew the short side of a triangle to the color #2 side of each 6-4-2 unit remaining from Step 20, orienting as shown. Press seams toward the triangle and trim off the extra dog-ear.

30. Use a ruler to draw a line between the ends of the seamlines. Sew on the line and trim off the excess. Press the seam in either direction and re-press the main seams toward BG.

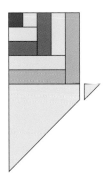

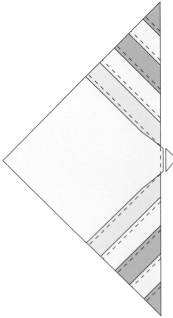

Draw line, sew, and trim.

34. Sew the short side of a second triangle to the other color #2 side of each square, orienting as shown.

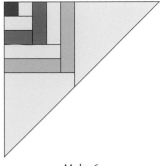

Make 6.

End Setting Triangles

Make 2 end setting triangles from colors #6, #4, and #2 and 4 from colors #5, #3, and #1. Instructions are for 6-4-2 triangles.

35. Sew together the long edges of a color #2 strip and a 2" BG strip. Press the seam toward the darker fabric. Subcut 4 segments to 9½".

36. Sew together the long edges of a color #4 strip and a 2" BG strip. Press the seam toward the darker fabric. Subcut 4 segments to 7".

37. From a 2" strip of color #6, cut 4 pieces 4". Use the remainder of the strip in Step 45.

38. From 2 BG 9½" strips, cut 6 squares 9½" × 9½". Set 4 aside to use in Step 42.

39. Sew the color #2 edge of a 9½" segment of color #2 + BG from Step 35 to one side of each square as shown below. Sew another segment from Step 35 to an adjacent side of each square in the same manner. Press seams toward color #2.

40. Add a 7" segment of color #4 + BG from Step 36 to the BG sides of the units. Press the seams either way.

41. Add a segment from Step 37 to the BG sides of the units as shown. Press toward BG. Repeat Steps 39–41 to make a second 6-4-2 unit.

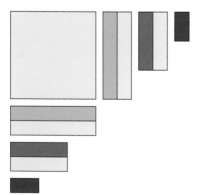

End setting triangles

42. Use the 4 remaining squares from Step 38, 4 BG 2" strips, 2 strips each of colors #1 and #3, and a 2" strip of color #5 to make 4 end setting triangles from colors #5, #3, and #1. Cut double the number of segments as in Steps 35–37.

Corners

43. Sew together the long edges of a color #2 strip and a 2" BG strip. Press seams toward the darker fabric. Subcut 4 segments to 9½".

44. Sew together the long edges of a color #4 strip and a 2" BG strip. Press seams toward the darker fabric. Subcut 4 segments to 7".

45. Cut 4 pieces 4" from a 2" strip of color #6.

46. Sew the color #2 side of a 9½" segment of color #2 + BG from Step 43 to a short side of each triangle left over from Step 32, orienting as shown. Be sure to orient 2 of the triangles in one direction and 2 in the other to obtain left and right corners. Press seams toward the triangle.

47. Sew the color #4 side of a 7" segment of color #4 + BG from Step 44 to the unit, orienting as shown. Press seams toward the darker fabric.

48. Sew a 4" segment of color #6 from Step 45 to the BG edge of each unit. Press seams toward BG.

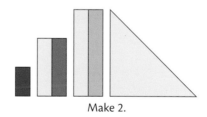

Make 2.

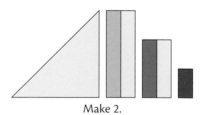

Make 2.

ASSEMBLY

The blocks are set on-point in this quilt, so you will sew rows on the diagonal. If possible, lay out the entire quilt before you start to sew, being especially careful with the side and end triangles. If any blocks are turned, your strips will not align, and the design will not flow. See the illustration.

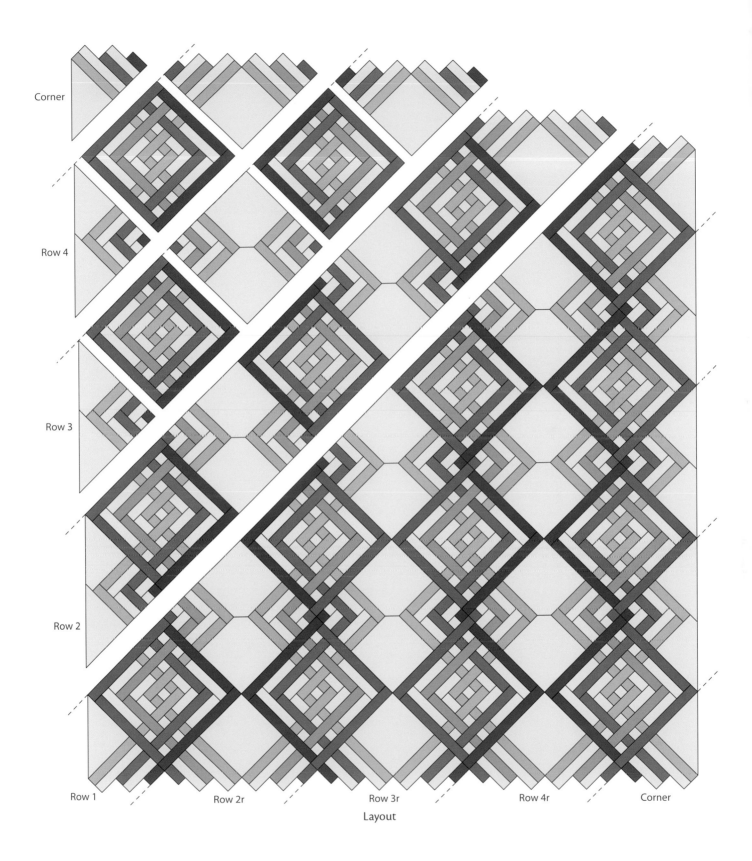

Corner

Row 4

Row 3

Row 2

Row 1

Row 2r

Row 3r

Row 4r

Corner

Layout

49. Make a row 1. Make 2 rows each of rows 2, 3, and 4. After you make each row 4, add a corner to each before continuing, making sure to use the correct corner.

50. Sew the rows together. Rows 2r, 3r, and 4r are rows 2, 3, and 4 that have been turned 180°.

51. Trim the top and bottom edges in a straight line ¼" outside the points of the main blocks. Do the same for the sides if necessary. Use a square ruler to make sure that the corners are square, but note that no seam meets the corner of the quilt. Staystitch the top and bottom (bias) edges about ⅛" from the raw edge.

FINISHING

52. For queen size, quilt and bind. For king size, add borders, quilt, and bind.

Scrappy Rat Race, 59" × 83"

The addition of the piano keys border livens up this smaller version.

BONUS PROJECT:
Amazing Maze

38" × 45½"

*T*he name of this quilt was derived from my satisfaction in discovering
that I could make another quilt from the leftovers of Rat Race (*page 67*).

FABRIC

Maze: Leftover pieced and unpieced strips from *Rat Race Neutrals* (page 67)

Borders: ⅝ yard

Backing: 1½ yards

Binding: ⅜ yard

Batting: 42″ × 50″

CUTTING

Maze

◆ As needed from scraps. See Construction.

Borders

◆ Cut 4 strips 4½″ × wof*.

* wof = width of fabric

CONSTRUCTION

The quilt uses 7½″ finished blocks that are set 4 × 5. You will need 8 straight blocks and 12 corner blocks.

Straight block

Corner block

Start by cutting the largest pieces you need from the largest scraps, disregarding their colors. Then cut smaller pieces from the remaining leftovers and from smaller scraps. Construct other pieces as needed from leftover strips and yardage. If you change the configuration, sketch out your idea and count the number of each type of block. Background fabric is referred to as BG.

1. Cut from scraps or construct 8 straight blocks from 2 color pieces and 3 BG pieces, each cut 2″ × 8″.

Save time by using parts of leftovers or by strip piecing 2″ strips from uncut fabric. For example, use the leftover pieces from Steps 4, 7, 8, and 10 of *Rat Race* (pages 69–70) by cutting down the large BG piece; measure 1¾″ from the existing seam to trim.

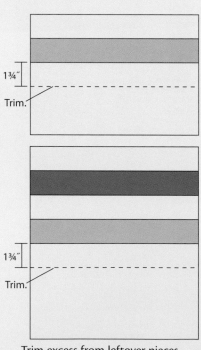

Trim excess from leftover pieces.

2. Cut from scraps or leftover fabric to construct 12 corner blocks as shown. For each of the 12 blocks, you need a 2″ segment of BG + any color; a 3½″ segment of BG + any color; a 5″ segment of BG + any color; a 6½″ segment of BG + any color; and a 2″ × 8″ segment of BG. Sew as shown, being sure to orient each segment correctly.

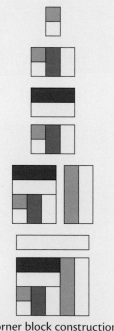

Corner block construction

3. Lay out the top in 5 rows of 4 blocks each, following the configuration in the photo.

4. Sew the blocks into rows and the rows into a top.

5. Add borders.

6. Layer, quilt, and bind.

ABOUT THE AUTHOR

Photo by Patricia E. Ritter

Jane Hardy Miller was taught to sew at the age of five by her mother, a home economics teacher. She made her first quilt in 1968, using the make-it-up-as-you-go method. She made quilts sporadically for the following ten years, then took a beginning quilting class and became obsessed. After making several hundred quilts, her primary quilting interests are now the use of color in quilts and the creation of three-dimensional effects in what is usually considered a two-dimensional medium.

Also by Jane Hardy Miller:

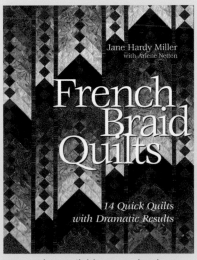

Also available as an ebook

Also available as an ebook

Great Titles *from* C&T PUBLISHING & STASH BOOKS

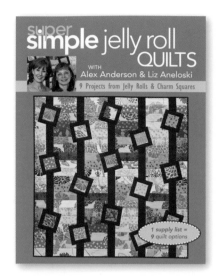

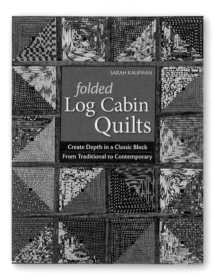

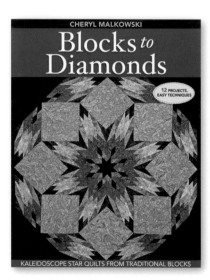

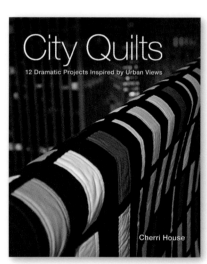

Available at your local retailer or **www.ctpub.com** *or* **800-284-1114**

For a list of other fine books from C&T Publishing, visit our website
to view our catalog online.

C&T PUBLISHING, INC.
P.O. Box 1456
Lafayette, CA 94549
800-284-1114

Email: ctinfo@ctpub.com
Website: www.ctpub.com

C&T Publishing's professional photography services are now available to
the public. Visit us at www.ctmediaservices.com.

Tips and Techniques can be found at www.ctpub.com > Consumer
Resources > Quiltmaking Basics: Tips & Techniques for Quiltmaking & More

For quilting supplies:

COTTON PATCH
1025 Brown Ave.
Lafayette, CA 94549
Store: 925-284-1177
Mail order: 925-283-7883

Email: CottonPa@aol.com
Website: www.quiltusa.com

Note: Fabrics used in the quilts shown may not be currently
available, as fabric manufacturers keep most fabrics in print for
only a short time.